HIKING ON THE
EDGE

WEST COAST TRAIL
JUAN DE FUCA TRAIL

HIKING ON THE

EDGE

IAN GILL
photographs by DAVID NUNUK

REVISED EDITION
EXPANDED AND UPDATED

RAINCOAST BOOKS
Vancouver

First edition published in 1995

Second edition published in 1998 by
Raincoast Books
8680 Cambie Street
Vancouver, B.C. v6p 6m9
(604) 323-7100

10 9 8 7 6 5 4 3 2 1

HENDERSON BOOK SERIES NO. 25

Published in association with the Canadian Parks and Wilderness Society. The Henderson Book Series honours the kind and generous support of Mrs. Arthur T. Henderson, whose commitment to building public support for parks and wilderness protection has made the series possible.

CANADIAN CATALOGUING IN PUBLICATION DATA

Gill, Ian, 1955-
Hiking on the edge

(Raincoast journeys)
ISBN 1-55192-146-4

1. Hiking – British Columbia – West Coast Trail. 2. Hiking – British Columbia – Juan de Fuca Trail. 3. West Coast Trail (B.C.) – Description and travel. 4. Juan de Fuca Trail (B.C.) – Description and travel. I. Nunuk, David. II. Title. III. Series.

FC3814.P3G54 1998   917.11'2   C97-910991-4
F1089.V3G54 1998

Printed in Hong Kong

CONTENTS

ACKNOWLEDGEMENTS

BOTH THE PHOTOGRAPHER AND THE AUTHOR ARE DEEPLY indebted to a number of people who got this project off the ground, guided it along the way, and pushed it to completion. First, we'd like to acknowledge Ken Budd of SummerWild Productions, who brought the two of us together under Raincoast's umbrella. We also owe a great debt to Jerry and Janet Etzkorn, and their kids Jake and Justine, for taking us in at the Carmanah Point Lighthouse; likewise Doug and Gwen Fraser for their unfailing hospitality at the Pachena Point Lighthouse. Thanks to Rod Nelson and Captain Terry Webber of the Canadian Coast Guard. And to the crew at Raincoast: Mark Stanton for his vision and enthusiasm; Michael Carroll for his editorial finesse; art director Dean Allen for so ably blending photos and type; and finally, Heather Wardle, the true backbone of this project, whose diligence and good grace kept us all hiking down the same trail.

The photographer would like to single out Delia Star and Robert Pilloud, who posed diligently under sometimes trying circumstances, and packed along some of the camera gear for their pains. He also wants to acknowledge the Qwa-Ba-Diwa for "saving my butt" during a particularly trying photo session when a storm caught him without a tent, or any food to speak of. Thanks should also go out to Bob

Tsusiat Falls: Natives once lowered their canoes over the falls and set forth on the ocean.

Herger, who was there even before Ken Budd. And finally, he would like to thank fellow photographer, friend, mentor, and ever-flowing vessel of benevolence Tom Kitchin for bestowing his wisdom and advice upon him.

The author is indebted to a number of people: Ron Hooper, park superintendent, and Rick Holmes, backcountry manager of Pacific Rim National Park, for helping get us on the trail and for comments on the manuscript; Jamie Morton for his insights into the trail's history; Bryan Cofsky for advice about the Ditidaht; and Ken Jones of the Pacheedaht Band. I'm particularly grateful to Richard Inglis and James Haggarty, whose ethnographic history of the park proved invaluable; and to Randy Bouchard of the British Columbia Indian Language Project, for his guidance on language and place names. I'd also like to thank Liz and Mike Hicks of Tyee Lodge in Bamfield, for a trail's end turkey sandwich and for their continuing hospitality. Lastly I owe a great deal to my partner, Jennifer Jordan – for her arch critiques, her unfailing good humour, and her loving support. She, and our young son Jasper, tolerate my absences and, when I'm home, the long hours spent handcuffed to the computer. So, for my part, this book is dedicated to Jennifer, and wee Jasper.

A pocket of beach near Nitinat Narrows.

THIS IS A CHRONICLE OF A JOURNEY; ACTUALLY, OF SEVERAL
journeys photographer Dave Nunuk and I have made to the West Coast
Trail. It is also a discourse on the history of the trail and the territory it
crosses. Doing justice to the trail, in words and pictures, demands more than a cur-
sory familiarity with the place. Dave has humped his cameras back and forth along
the trail too many times to count. He's also taken too many pictures to count,
although he guesses more than 8,000 frames passed across his light table in the two
years it took him to bring the trail home on film (they've been edited down to 64
for this project). For my part, I've made several trips to the trail at different times of
the year. Thus, while the book's prologue is set in the dying days of one hiking season, the main text of the book that follows is set at the very beginning of another
season. It would be foolhardy to call either experience "typical." No two hikes
along the West Coast Trail are the same; nor is there a universal reckoning of what
it's like to experience the place. Thousands of individual hikers take to the trail each
year – each will have their own adventures, their own epiphanies.

They come from all over the world to tackle what Parks Canada calls "one of
the most gruelling treks in North America." Expert hikers would scoff at the

description, given that the trail is maintained by wardens and construction crews and rarely climbs more than 100 feet above sea level. The trail attracts 8,000 hikers a year, hardly a purist's idea of untrodden wilderness. And yet, for all but the most experienced outdoorsman, the West Coast Trail is indeed gruelling. And to all but the most jaded eyes, it is spectacular. Stretched along 47 miles of some of the wildest coastline in the world, the trail is a necklace strung with matchless jewels: coves, beaches, bays, rivers, waterfalls, rock ledges, caves, tidal pools… an immensely complex littoral framed on one side by the sea and fringed on the other by remnants of one of the Earth's most magnificent temperate rainforests. Added to all this is the animal, marine, and bird life that only such a place, left largely undisturbed, can sustain.

That this sliver of forest remains unaltered is itself extraordinary. The trail hugs the southwestern shore of Vancouver Island, whose forests, for the most part, have been cannibalized through decades of overcutting and abuse. Preserving the trail was an early battle and a rare victory for common sense in a corner of the universe that has attracted worldwide infamy. Just up the coast from here is Clayoquot Sound, a sublimely beautiful area that has been savaged and, in large measure, surrendered to

Ladders plunge through remnants of one of the Earth's greatest rainforests.

a combination of greed and ignorance. And those same industrial conceits have been practised just a stone's throw away from the trail itself. From the air you can see logging operations pressing hard against the narrow buffer of trees through which the trail is strung. Even if you don't fly over the trail, driving to either end of it gives the uninitiated a very quick lesson in the *realpolitik* that governs British Columbia life. Here are clearcuts, log booms, mills, and all the muscular infrastructure that has taken a heavy toll from the land. Given industry's insatiable appetite for "fibre," and its reflexive antipathy toward parks, it's amazing that the West Coast Trail is here at all. But it is, protected for all time as part of Canada's Pacific Rim National Park.

The park was established in 1970 after a momentous battle to have the coastline preserved. Many of the shibboleths we hear today about jobs versus the environment were forged back then in the heated battle to thwart the companies from logging Vancouver Island clear to the shoreline. As early as 1926, the area around Nitinat Lake and along the southwest coast had been recognized for its recreational potential and set aside as a park reserve. But as the companies got hungrier the designation was overturned in 1947 and the region was opened to logging, ostensibly because it was too remote for recreation. It was supposed to be an area where only small operators could log, but the majors got their way and by the mid-sixties the forests were included in Tree Farm Licences 44 and 46. At about the same time the logging companies began their most determined incursions into the region, having almost deforested the areas closer to their mills. Obviously they saw no reason why they shouldn't just log Vancouver Island from mountaintop to shoreline.

But along the southwestern shoreline of British Columbia were the remnants of an old lifesaving trail, built after the turn of the century to aid shipwrecked mariners. By the 1960s the lifesaving trail had fallen into disuse and disrepair, but as the logging companies bore down on the coast an outdoor recreation boom took hold and people began to hike the trail again. Provincial park workers even helped clear it in stretches. People hiked, liked what they saw, and didn't like what the logging companies had in mind. A rump preservation movement began to call for the coast's protection. In 1968 there was a proposal to create a national historic trail centred around the sites of the old shipwrecks. That didn't take root, but the grow-ing clamour to set aside the trail simply for its natural wonders was heard in faraway Ottawa. In April 1970, when Pacific Rim National Park was established, its south-ernmost portion embraced the West Coast Trail.

The creation of the park required the consent of the B.C. government, which passed enabling legislation on March 20, 1969. That set off a storm of controversy over what the boundaries of the new park would be, and before the year was out rumours circulated that the province might renege on the arrangement. The Sierra Club headed an intense lobbying effort to keep both governments honest, and in 1970 then Northern Development Minister Jean Chrétien signed the park into being. The boundaries were to be settled at a later date and, in 1971, the Sierra Club weighed in with a compelling 35-page "plea for wider boundaries." It got them in 1972 when both the trail preserve was widened and the Nitinat Lakes region was embraced by the park.

In 1971, just a year after being signed into being, the park welcomed more than 2,000 hikers. Twenty years later almost 10,000 registered hikers made the trek from Port Renfrew to Bamfield, or vice versa. The explosion of interest, and the subse-quent pressure on the trail, forced Parks Canada, in 1991, to institute a quota on the number of hikers who could take to the trail each year. The West Coast Trail is now world-renowned and, closer to home, Pacific Rim National Park is still celebrated as an important early victory for British Columbia's now battle-weary environ-mentalists. However, there hasn't been much cheering by Native people.

Amply recorded in every account of the West Coast Trail is the fact that it was built to aid mariners who fell prey to the treacherous waters of the Strait of Juan de Fuca. What is seldom noted is that the entire trail crosses territory to which Native people lay claim. "They just went ahead and established the trail. That's trespass right there," says Ken Jones, elected chief of the Pacheedaht band in Port Renfrew. The eastern end of the trail is in Pacheedaht territory, the central section is in Ditidaht ter-ritory, and the Ohiaht people's territory embraces the western end of the trail around Bamfield. The three bands formed the Quu'as West Coast Trail Group in 1995, a joint venture that has since contracted with Pacific Rim National Park to provide six trail "guardians" during the season. The guardians, two per territory, offer a variety of services, including maintenance, ensuring compliance with park regulations, aiding in rescues, and the protection and interpretation of cultural resources. The motivation, according to Bryan Cofsky, speaking for the Ditidaht, was to derive some economic benefit from the park and "to create some sort of aboriginal content within the trail."

And why not? European contact along Canada's West Coast is barely 200 years old, yet the original inhabitants, collectively known as the Nuu-chah-nulth people, are thought to have inhabited the coast for as long as 4,300 years. By all accounts they were a rough bunch, not given to much of what we would call hiking. When the Nuu-chah-nulth wanted to roam beyond their villages, they did so mainly in imposing cedar canoes. They fought hard, often over whaling rights, and sometimes settled their grievances through the exchange of women. They were beset by natural disasters – floods, earthquakes, tidal waves, landslides – but the West Coast was a well-stocked larder and, as hard as life must have been, the Nuu-chah-nulth fed, clothed, and sheltered themselves and still found time for art and invention. Constant battles between themselves and against the elements meant that the Nuu-chah-nulth were robust and entirely self-sufficient. But they were no match for the coming of the white man.

Hikers in the mist: Natives preferred to paddle.

Slabs of sandstone just west of Carmanah Point.

Spaniards aboard the *Santiago* made first contact with the Nuu-chah-nulth (or "Nootka" people, as they were wrongly called for decades) in Nootka Sound in 1774. Three years later the *Imperial Beagle* hove to off the coast farther south at Barkley Sound, named after Captain Charles Barkley, the ship's commander. Apparently Barkley saw but did not enter the Strait of Juan de Fuca. But one year later Robert Duffin did enter the strait in a longboat off the *Felice Adventurer,* captained by John Meares. On July 14 Duffin and 13 men "steered . . . along the coast, at a distance of a quarter of a mile. This coast, in general, to a village called Nittee Natt, affords a very pleasant prospect. . . ." Duffin tried to cross the bar at the mouth of what we now know as Nitinat Narrows, but the surf was too high. On July 16 Duffin spied a village and "immediately on our approaching the shore, the natives assembled on the beach with spears, bludgeons, bows and arrows making at the same time a dismal howling. . . ." The next day the longboat drew alongside several canoes bristling with weapons. There were also armed people in the trees along the shore. Duffin ordered his men to fire, and "we instantly had a shower of arrows poured on us from shore." No one was mortally wounded, and Duffin beat a retreat to the *Felice Adventurer.*

In 1788 the *Washington* plied the strait, passing "Nitenat" and reaching Port San Juan. The "smoak of the Natives habitation" was seen at the head of the bay, wrote an officer named Haswell. "I believe we are the first Vessel that was ever in this port. . . . This place by the natives is called Patchenat and by us Poverty Cove." Poverty or not, there was a rich trade to be done along the coast, especially in furs. Ships became regular fixtures along the coast, exchanging copper, clothing, and trifles for valuable sea otter pelts. Thus began a sometimes congenial but mostly fractious and unequal relationship between the original inhabitants of the coast and foreign plunderers, who often came unstuck in the Strait of Juan de Fuca. Europeans would eventually come to build their lifesaving trail to aid their shipwrecked mariners. They would let it fall into disuse and then revive it as a hiking trail. But it pays to remember that the trail has always been a source of bemusement, often distress, for the original inhabitants of the territories it intersects.

That said, where else in the world, if anywhere, can one hike a trail that is as wild and far-flung as the West Coast Trail and yet so steeped in history? There are few ready comparisons. In England you can wander along the Pennine Way, "the longest footpath in Britain," as it's been described. Five times as long as the West Coast Trail, it passes through the Wuthering Heights of Brontë country, along Hadrian's Wall, and through endless bogs and moorland. But there's usually a pub at the end of most days, and lodgings if the weather turns foul. In short, it can be woolly but never really wild. In Switzerland you can hike between *Hüttes* dotted among the 10,000-foot peaks above Zermatt; in Austria, pitch your *Zelt* (tent) in the Alps…spectacular places usually with crowds to match. In the ethereal heights of Nepal you can strike out from Pokhara for the Annapurna Sanctuary and spend memorable days tracing the hemline of great mountains. In South America, despite Jorge Luis Borges's contention that "There is nothing in Patagonia," there are, in fact, marvellous hikes among the volcanoes and glaciers of the Patagonian Andes, and in the plentiful forests of southern beech. But nowhere in Europe, in Asia, in South America, indeed nowhere else in North America, is there a hike quite like the West Coast Trail. New Zealand comes close, but its four-day Milford Track is fairly tame and notoriously crowded. The Australian state of Tasmania offers the Overland Track, but its huts get jammed with people in the peak season. Tasmania's South West National Park has some tough hiking along its coast, and probably most closely rivals what Vancouver Island's western shore has to offer, which is a rare chance to wander along the fault line that separates land from sea, with nothing intersecting your path other than rivers and streams racing to slake the ocean's thirst. It is true there are crowds on the West Coast Trail, too. But there are no pubs, no peaks, no porters, just a long, hard walk for anyone game to try it and willing to marry themselves to a heavy pack for a week or more.

While there's no typical hike, there are some fundamentals common to everyone's turn along this track. For instance, the most basic decision is which way to hike the trail. Deciding what end to start at is a little like deciding how to enter a swimming pool. Do you plunge in at the deep end, or wade in slowly at the shallow end? The deep end in this case is the "bottom" end, or eastern entry point at Port Renfrew, a small coastal community about a two-hour drive west of Victoria. The bottom end is far and away the toughest stretch of the trail, and if you plunge headlong onto the trail at the Renfrew end, the assumption is that you're fit enough and tough enough to endure its rigours with next to no adjustment. People who need a little conditioning are best off starting at Bamfield, which is reached by road from Victoria, or by water or road from Port Alberni. Starting in Bamfield allows people to work their way into the trail's rhythms and moods, gaining a little fitness for the tough slogging to come. Whether it speaks to some deep-seated propensity for self-abuse, or perhaps reveals an excess of misplaced machismo, I've always started the trail at the Renfrew end. That's where Dave Nunuk and I kicked off a journey we thought was worth sharing.

Deep in the forest, steeped in history.

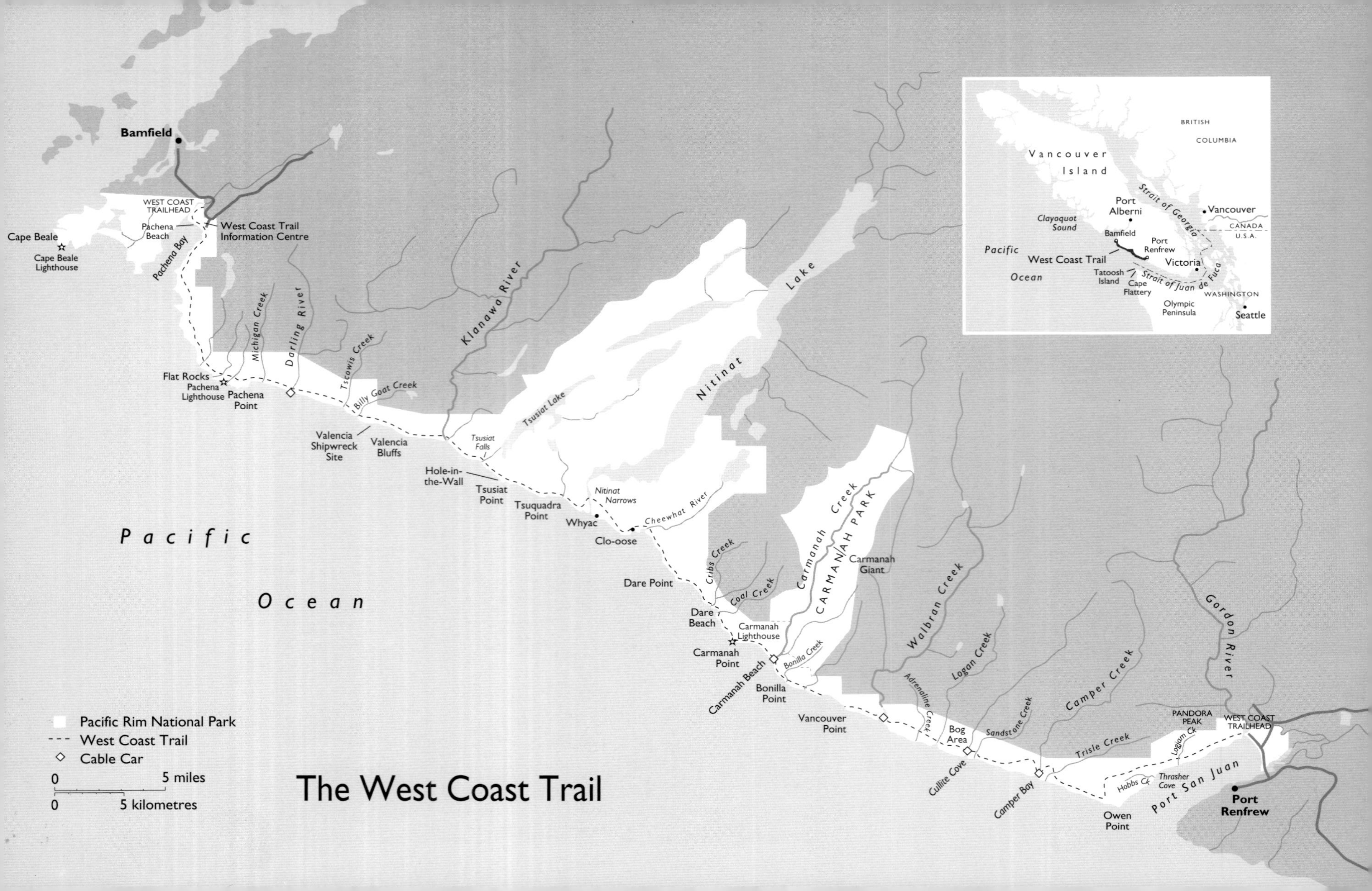
The West Coast Trail
Pacific Rim National Park
West Coast Trail
Cable Car
0 5 miles
0 5 kilometres
Pacific
Ocean
Bamfield
Cape Beale
Cape Beale Lighthouse
WEST COAST TRAILHEAD
Pachena Beach
Pachena Bay
West Coast Trail Information Centre
Michigan Creek
Darling River
Flat Rocks
Pachena Lighthouse
Pachena Point
Tscowis Creek
Billy Goat Creek
Klanawa River
Valencia Shipwreck Site
Valencia Bluffs
Tsusiat Falls
Tsusiat Lake
Hole-in-the-Wall
Tsusiat Point
Tsuquadra Point
Nitinat Lake
Nitinat Narrows
Whyac
Clo-oose
Cheewhat River
Dare Point
Cribs Creek
Coal Creek
Dare Beach
Carmanah Lighthouse
Carmanah Point
Carmanah Beach
Carmanah Creek
CARMANAH PARK
Carmanah Giant
Bonilla Creek
Bonilla Point
Vancouver Point
Walbran Creek
Adrenaline Creek
Logan Creek
Bog Area
Sandstone Creek
Cullite Cove
Camper Creek
Camper Bay
Trisle Creek
PANDORA PEAK
Logjam Ck
Hobbs Ck
Thrasher Cove
Owen Point
Port San Juan
Gordon River
WEST COAST TRAILHEAD
Port Renfrew
BRITISH COLUMBIA
Vancouver Island
Strait of Georgia
Vancouver
CANADA
U.S.A.
Port Alberni
Clayoquot Sound
Bamfield
Port Renfrew
Pacific Ocean
West Coast Trail
Victoria
Tatoosh Island
Cape Flattery
Strait of Juan de Fuca
WASHINGTON
Olympic Peninsula
Seattle

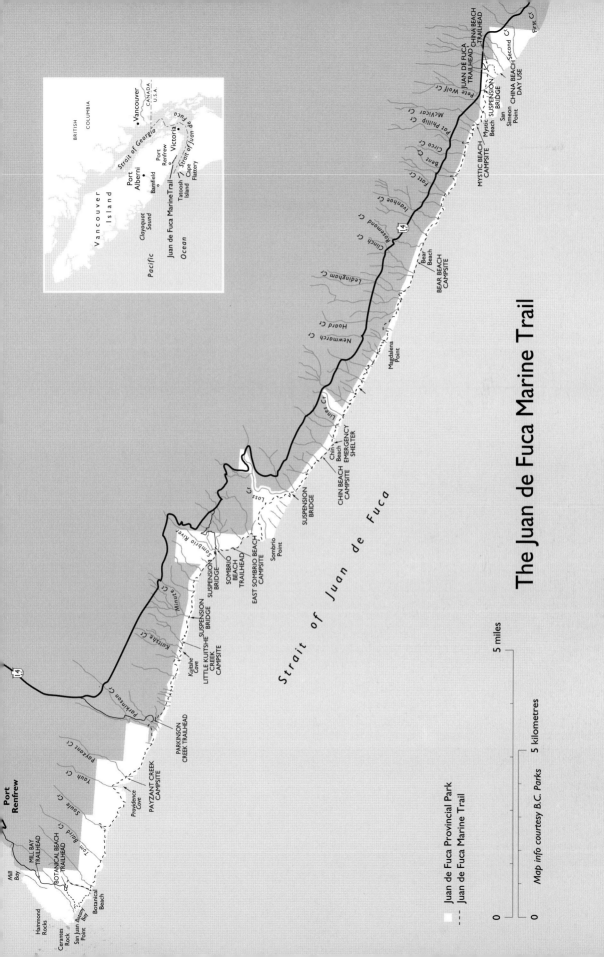

The Juan de Fuca Marine Trail

BRITISH COLUMBIA

CANADA
U.S.A.

Vancouver

Strait of Georgia

Vancouver Island

Port Alberni

Bamfield

Port Renfrew

Victoria

Tatoosh Island
Cape Flattery

Strait of Juan de Fuca

Juan de Fuca Marine Trail

Pacific Ocean

Clayoquot Sound

Strait of Juan de Fuca

Mill Bay

Hammond Rocks

Cerantes Rock

San Juan Point
Beamy Bay

Botanical Beach

MILL BAY TRAILHEAD

BOTANICAL BEACH TRAILHEAD

Tom Baird Cr

Soule Cr

Youb Cr

Providence Cove

Polzont Cr

PAYZANT CREEK CAMPSITE

Parkinson Cr

PARKINSON CREEK TRAILHEAD

Minute Cr

Kuitshe Cr

Kuitshe Cove

LITTLE KUITSHE CREEK CAMPSITE

SUSPENSION BRIDGE

Sombrio River

SUSPENSION BRIDGE

SOMBRIO BEACH TRAILHEAD

EAST SOMBRIO BEACH CAMPSITE

Sombrio Point

Loss Cr

SUSPENSION BRIDGE

Chin Beach

CHIN BEACH CAMPSITE

CHIN BEACH EMERGENCY SHELTER

Lines Cr

Magdalena Point

Newmarch Cr

Hoard Cr

Ledingham Cr

Clinch Cr

Rosemond Cr

Bear Beach

BEAR BEACH CAMPSITE

Ivanhoe Cr

Fatt Cr

14

Bent Cr

Circo Cr

Port Phillip Cr

Pete Wolf Cr

MYSTIC BEACH CAMPSITE

Mystic Beach

Simeon Point

JUAN DE FUCA TRAILHEAD

JUAN DE FUCA TRAILHEAD

SUSPENSION BRIDGE

San SUSPENSION BRIDGE

CHINA BEACH TRAILHEAD

CHINA BEACH DAY USE

Second Cr

First Cr

14

Port Renfrew

Juan de Fuca Provincial Park

- - - Juan de Fuca Marine Trail

Map info courtesy B.C. Parks

5 miles

5 kilometres

0

0

S TANDING ON A SLAB OF RUST-COLOURED ROCK, AS IF ON THE deck of a huge ship in a storm, I instinctively recoil as the autumnal pulse of the Pacific spends itself at my feet. Waves arrive in platoons, their broad green shoulders edged with foam epaulets. They march resolutely toward the shore, exploding onto the rocks with the booming authority of artillery. There's a menacing roar, a great firestorm of broken water... but the rock holds and the seawater turns turtle and rushes back into itself, as if embarrassed by its own hyperbole.

The rock absorbs wave after wave, blow after blow, with no obvious effect. But on closer inspection it is evident that the sandstone has been pockmarked by infinite, insistent rivulets of water. It looks like a lava bed, stamped with what could be mistaken for animal prints in the rock, or the petroglyphs of a lost tribe. Actually, it is all the work of the sea, writing epitaphs in stone, then busily rewriting them, never quite content to let the shoreline rest in peace.

Closer to the base of the cliff, rock stanchions thrust off the deck, sandstone stalagmites that seem to invite a rope, to offer purchase, somewhere to tether the storm. But there is no rope, just thick bullwhips of kelp tossed up in clumps along the shore. The cliffs themselves are overhung with moss-covered branches, suspended like

The Pacific's pulse: all the force of nature funnelled at your feet.

I

bushy eyebrows frowning over the maelstrom below. At my feet are deep rock pools, each a teeming aquarium of busy tidal life that seems oblivious to the hell-broth boil and bubble of the incoming tide.

This is just one place, one small pocket of shoreline west of Carmanah Point. Mariners have a word for such a tiny inlet; they call it a "gut." There are places just like this all along the West Coast Trail. Stand at any one of them during an incoming tide and you'll swear all the force of nature is funnelled at your feet. In fact, scenes very similar to this one are playing out along the length of the coast, although no two scenes are exactly the same and most of them play to an empty house. They are unobserved and unrecorded, except for those days when hikers make their pilgrimage to these shores to pay homage to nature and to top up their depleted souls.

Toward the end of this particular day the waves stand at attention beneath a corpulent sun which, late in the season, starts to hide its last rays behind a bank of clouds on the horizon soon after 6:00 p.m. The day has been clear, windy but sunny. Suddenly it turns bitterly cold. The noise from the surf blanks out all but the wheeling cries of a few gulls, and the whooping coughs of sea lions that have colonized a chip of rock in the near distance. I look in either direction along the shore, but for once there are no other hikers to share the spectacle. So I listen all alone to the thunderous report of surf hitting the rocks, all that energy, that fury, instilling me with an almost hypnotic sense of calm.

I barely notice that an inky darkness has begun to stain the sky, and it's only when my feet get drenched by a wave that I realize the tide has begun to flood. My reverie broken, I hustle around the point and walk briskly back to my camp on Carmanah Beach. Soon a sour-smelling fire of driftwood competes with the chill of the night air. Off in the distance the Carmanah Point lighthouse looks like Disney's Fantasyland hoisted out on the bluff. It blinks comfortingly, and soon, so do the stars. After dinner sleep quickly takes command and holds sway till early in the morning when the foghorn of the Carmanah lighthouse sounds its basso profundo, like a booming alarm clock. Looking out from my tent, I see that Fantasyland has gone, swallowed by fog. There's a dusting of frost on the sand, and over everything else, like icing sugar. Soon there is hot coffee and the promise of food and already the morning sun is sending pale fingers of warmth through the treetops. It is another splendid morning on the West Coast Trail, and just being here is its own reward. Out here, every day is a gift.

A Steller's jay takes a moment's rest.

T IS 1:40 P.M. ON THE FIRST DAY OF THE HIKING SEASON, MAY 1.
We're standing on the rocks near the mouth of the Gordon River, yelling our
thanks and our goodbyes to the skipper of a boat that has just ferried us to the
trailhead for five bucks a head. I've been here, done this before, and I'm not all that
deliriously happy about what the immediate future holds. Earlier Dave and I had
petitioned several people in Port Renfrew, trying to get someone to drop us off at
Thrasher Cove, which is three trail miles away from where we now stand, and a
much more agreeable "in" point. This early in the season, however, the seas are still
running too high and no one will risk their boat on the rocks no matter what
inducements we proffer. Everyone laughs us off. Eventually we're forced to aban-
don all prospect of a shortcut and, after taking a quick hop across the Gordon River,
we're dumped at the trailhead. We have fully 47 miles stretching between us and
Bamfield. This late in the day we aim to take just three off the total.

The hike to Thrasher Cove is not the most memorable part of our journey, but
it does help orient one to the trail's peculiarities. After just 10 minutes of hiking, we
come across the first trace of the old telegraph wire that once ran the length of this
coast. It was a vital lifeline for mariners who washed up on these shores, and for the

"One of the most gruelling treks in North America."

5

hardy folk who settled out here. The wire in some places is still strung between glass insulators, which are attached to trees alongside the trail. In some places the wire disappears altogether, torn down by falling trees and passing time. It's just a remnant now, but what urgent messages must have once raced along its length, signalling catastrophe and calamity and demanding quick action from Victoria.

It being spring, thickets of salmonberry are in flower, which is welcome news for hummingbirds; later, the berries themselves will be out. Also now, the brilliant yellow of skunk cabbage dots either side of the trail in its swampier sections. Bears will feed on the skunk cabbage as they emerge from hibernation, too early yet for their preferred diet of berries. Wherever there's a dead tree here, there's usually a bracket fungus. When we stop to catch our breath at one point, I spy a bracket fungus the size of a serving platter, a great big knot of spongy mould welded to a tree trunk like a mussel to a rock. After 45 minutes, we confront "L35," a park designation for one of the many ladders that carry hikers down into steep gullies and back

That was then: the road that once ran from Bamfield to Pachena Point, and soon surrendered to the elements. Now it's the easiest stretch of the West Coast Trail.

out again. This ladder is indeed steep, but fairly short. The next one is even shorter, "L34" having surrendered its bottom section to a swollen stream. Park wardens and repair crews do what they can to maintain the trail's structures – bridges, ladders, boardwalks, cable cars – but this is wild country, and hikers can't assume that every time a tree or a stream wipes out a stretch of trail, someone will be on hand to immediately fix it. In this instance, with little effort, Dave and I manage to scale the rock face and hitch back onto what's left of the ladder. Little do we know that this is just a taste of what's to come.

For the most part, the trail is in good shape in the early going, although it cuts through a scrappy second-growth forest, which is decidedly less interesting than old-growth. In an old-growth forest, the forest floor is much more open and inviting, the trees more stately. Here the undergrowth is a lot more tangled and the trees much less grand – a work in progress that hasn't yet achieved the sober majesty of old-growth. On either side of the trail, however, it's possible to see huge stumps from the loggers' first pass through this territory. Indeed, about halfway from the trailhead to Thrasher Cove we encounter an old Empire donkey engine, a hugely redundant-looking relic from the early logging operations here. Thick cables snake through the undergrowth like tentacles, and it's easy to imagine the awful strain, the wet and the dirt, the grinding Dickensian scene that must have played out here in order to get the big trees down and away.

The hiking gets hard in this patch. We skirt Pandora Peak, feeling a little like mountain goats, one side of our bodies always cocked uphill against the 45-degree rake of the land, a stance made that much harder by gravity's pull on our packs. The trail is entirely inland, and there is only one decent view of Port San Juan, which comes soon after the donkey engine. From this, the highest point on the entire trail (a mere 600 feet), we can see clear to the Olympic Peninsula in the United States. Two freighters slump toward port in the distance, and we can see a fair-size surf breaking across the inlet on the rocks off San Juan Point.

Three hours after our hike began we're at Logjam Creek. Fifteen minutes later we turn off the trail proper and head down toward the inviting sound of the sea.

Thrasher Cove comes to us courtesy of 101 precipitous steps on a ladder and, suddenly, we're at our first destination of the journey. My first thought, having dumped my pack on a log, is that Thrasher Cove is living up to its name. My second thought, watching the surf crash onto the shore, is that it's a good thing everyone convinced us to leave our bravado on the dock back at Port Renfrew. Landing off a boat here would not have been pretty. And, anyway, it somehow wouldn't have been honest to have begun a wilderness trek by doing the first three miles in a boat. So here we are, an afternoon's robust exercise under our belts, and possessed of a grand sense of moral superiority at having pulled our own weight to get here. That's the great thing about hiking – you can turn even the most pathetic accomplishment into a stellar tale of derring-do. And since it's so early in the season, there's no one here to tell us just how ordinary our afternoon's work has been.

We make a camp in a well-worn area beside Hobbs Creek. The sky is overcast, but rain looks unlikely. There's a good-size cave here in which, judging by the fire pit, others have camped in the past when the weather has turned sour. But we chance our hand and camp out, and soon have a healthy fire burning. The beach is choked with driftwood, so fuel is plentiful. There's always something mildly unsettling about the first night of a hike, especially when it's the opening hike of the season and the tent is out for the first time, and you worry about what you might have forgotten (or, in my case, if I've packed too much). There's a sort of settling-in period when, having opened the hike, you want it to decant for a while.

The other peculiarity about the first night of a hike is that it's a kind of decompression period, a sort of cushion between the softness of daily life and the rigours of the trail proper. In our case the cushion comes in the form of two lovely steaks, cooked by Dave over the campfire on stakes he's fashioned out of elderberry branches. I make an accompanying Maritime Pasta Supreme, or so the package calls it, and we wash the lot down with a bottle of 1990 Wolf Blass Cabernet Sauvignon (tinged with only the slightest taste of the plastic water bottle I'd transferred it into the night before). No doubt wilderness purists would wince at the decadence of it all, but it goes down like a charm.

Dare Beach and the natural shield of rock known as the Cribs.

I remember that I've been here before. The first time I hiked the trail was in 1988, with an American friend who was living in Paris, and an Australian friend who was living in London. We, too, had tried to get a boat ride to Thrasher Cove, in our case in late September, also to no avail. We, too, had hiked the first three miles and set up camp here. That night four sodden and sullen Norwegian women were camped beside us, having hiked seven days and camped six nights in cold, driving rain. Norwegians, Americans, Australians, Germans ... of the maximum 8,000 hikers who can register to hike the trail every year, about a quarter are foreigners. For some it's the principal reason they come to British Columbia. For many it's the wildest place they've ever been, or will ever be.

Sitting by the fire on the first night, Dave and I can see the lights of Port Renfrew twinkling across the oily dark heave of Port San Juan. A Native legend tells of this place and a pivotal moment in its history: "One morning sea foam filled the village at the head of Port San Juan. The chief sent out an old slave woman to see if it was safe, which it was. They took on the name *P'aachiidʔ* which meant 'sea foam' after this event, and became a separate people." Thus the *P'aachiidʔaaʔtx* or Pacheedaht people came into being centuries ago, splitting from the Ditidaht people, who moved farther up the coast. This all took place "at an unknown time in the past," and the area has been Pacheedaht territory ever since. Thrasher Cove itself was one of five permanent settlements, a village of eight houses known as *O:yats'* or "bay facing in the bay."

Our camp looks out on the bay where, in 1788, the crew of the *Washington* must have strained to see the "smoak of the Natives habitation" at the head of the bay, where Port Renfrew now sits, its lights decorating the edge of the rainforest. Whether or not this stretch of water deserved to be called Poverty Bay, the Pacheedaht people certainly fell on hard times after contact with Europeans. They, like Natives all along the coast, traded in pelts, although relatively few ships bothered to risk this stretch of coast. From 1785 to 1825 there were about 300 ship voyages to the Northwest Coast, but only about 15 of those were to the rugged shores of what is now the West Coast Trail. However, by the 1840s trading patterns had started to change. Instead of lingering for the shortest time possible to conduct an exchange, traders began looking to develop the area commercially and to establish settlements. Port San Juan was one of the earliest. In 1854 William Eddy Banfield, Peter Francis, and Thomas Laughton operated a small trading schooner and actually had a store at Port San Juan. The main commodity then was dogfish oil. The main effect on the West Coast Indians, however, was "the venereal" and "that scourge of mankind the Smallpox," according to records from the *Columbia*. By the time Captain Robert Brown mounted an expedition down the coast in 1864, he was prompted to write that the Pacheedaht were "once a principal tribe...but with war and disease they are now so thinned that they have amalgamated with the Nitinats."

Dave and I are now so thinned by the efforts of the day that we amalgamate with our sleeping bags, trusting that we won't wake to a tent full of sea foam.

Rest for the wicked after the first day's tough slogging.

A CROW DOES THE WORK OF A ROOSTER IN THE MORNING AT Thrasher Cove, and soon we're creaking around the campsite, working stiffness and cold out of our limbs. Dave walks down to the water's edge and surprises a river otter, which wriggles gamely off the sand and slurps back into the surf. Up by the camp a hummingbird feeds on salmonberry flowers while we make short work of flapjacks and syrup. We are hiking by 10:00 a.m., keen to get to Owen Point for an appointment with low tide at 11:00.

A Scotch mist clings to the air as we begin an hour of uncertain scrambling over slippery serpentine boulders, tossed like huge dice onto the shore. Because we've been blessed with a late-morning low tide, we're able to turn our backs on the 101 steps back up to the trail. Instead, today's trek will be a beach hike. In the past I've missed the tide and had to climb up out of Thrasher Cove and go inland again, which is no more distinguished a hike than the first three miles. So it's a boon to be able to strike a path along the coastline so early in the trip.

All the same, the rocks are slick from the mist and still wet from high tide. Most of them are also coated in algae. Every step is a potential broken ankle, or worse,

The shelf at Owen Point: at low tide as greasy as a skillet.

13

A bald eagle that deigned to pose for us.

and the extra weight on our backs emphasizes the commitment behind every footfall. It's tense, tricky work. As our boots seek a purchase, crabs scuttle out from underfoot, and I gain an appreciation for why they're designed the way they are, and why you don't see *them* backpacking a third of their body weight over a slimy boulder.

Just before Owen Point we come across the stern of a trawler. Who knows how long it's been here? The steel hull is bent and rusted, but the wooden decking is surprisingly intact. This was a big boat and, judging by how convincingly it has been deposited on the rocks, its career came to a violent end. Indeed the West Coast Trail owes its origins not just to the telegraph line strung up in 1888-89, but to a series of marine tragedies around the turn of the century that earned this stretch of coast the sobriquet, "Graveyard of the Pacific." In 1906, after one tragedy too many, an indolent bureaucracy finally upgraded the telegraph trail, and in the decades to come the "Lifesaving Trail," or "Shipwrecked Mariner's Trail," was a vital component of the Pacific coast's rescue infrastructure. After clambering over the grave of this particular victim for a few minutes, we take a cold draught of water from Cleft Falls, dump our packs, and set about exploring Owen Point. It is exactly 11:00 a.m., so the tide is as low as it's going to get.

We wander light-footed among evolutionary rock sculptures on the sandstone shelf, which the receding waters have left as greasy as a skillet. Much of the shelf is carpeted with algae so bright green that it looks as if a country club groundskeeper has been a little heavy-handed with the fertilizer. An eagle circles, so we tarry in an attempt to get a good photograph, but this isn't a great place to linger too long. The tide is out, but that means the water has only one way to go, and we have a long way to go along the shelf before we'll rejoin the inland trail. Still, we spend a few minutes more examining a huge cleavage in the cliff and discover two gaping sea arches where the waves have pounded holes in the cliff. Standing behind the arches, each the size of a huge movie screen, we look out toward the sea and are given a private screening of a dynamic, ever-changing scene.

At Owen Point there's also a huge sea stack, one of those almost Gothic islets of rock, usually capped with a few forlorn trees, and usually surrounded by surging water at high tide. This particular point marks where the coast trail turns out of Port San Juan and adopts the east-west axis that it follows to the end. Given the way Vancouver Island shoulders against the North American mainland, it's common to think of this coastline as being on a north-south orientation, but as deceptive as things might seem, we set out from here, heading more west than north. There are no longer any big boulders to impede our progress, and we pick up the pace. In comparison to the previous day's work in the woods, this is a delight: the shelf is flat and hard under foot. To our left, the sea bristles and heaves; to our right, the forest breathes deeply. We cut a purposeful line between the two. The stiffness is gone

The big screen: sea arch at Owen Point.

from our legs, our packs have settled, and we seem to draw a constant pulse of energy from the teeming picture in which we find ourselves framed.

The shelf is not without its own deceits. At times it is intersected by deep crevasses, surge channels that for the most part are narrow enough to jump across. There's no margin for error here, though. Each abyss is maybe 15 feet deep, and the rock walls are concave and as smooth as a gun barrel. Falling in would be easy; getting out would be a nightmare. One large surge channel sends a rush of air inland, which spends itself in an underground rock hollow with the lusty boom of a bass drum. Another cuts too deep and too wide to breach with a single leap, so we hike up into the thick wall of salal, a tough shrub with dark purple berries that hedges

this entire length of coast. An opening has been cut in the salal, and we dodge around behind the surge channel and move on.

We lope along the shelf, or as it's popularly known, the "moonscape," for another mile before we reach a rack of massive cliffs, the rock scooped smooth and concave by the surf. The brow of rock hangs over us like a frown, and the sea itself now looks sterner: the incoming tide is tossing waves closer and closer to our boots, and this is clearly no place to be when the ocean's dander is up. The Scotch mist, meanwhile, has turned to decidedly Canadian rain. At 1:30, three and a half hours after we set out from Thrasher Cove, and about four miles farther along, we've walked as far as the shelf will take us. We climb onto a high knoll, where the trail dives back into the bush, and eat a granola-bar lunch. There's just a glimpse of sun as we rest for a while, looking down from safely on high as the tide reclaims our temporary trail and erases all hint of our having been there.

It's a steep, two-rope grunt back onto the trail proper. We're in old-growth forest now, and the trail is a lot prettier than the first leg. The forest floor is less

Hiking on the ledge: the author just west of Owen Point.

cluttered with debris and undergrowth, the trees much more stolid and substantial. There are four main species of big trees along this coast: Douglas fir, western hemlock, western red cedar, and the magnificent Sitka spruce. Viewed from the shoreline, the dominant species is the Sitka spruce, rising high up out of the salal, hedged with scrappy alder trees that are bearded with delicate pale bluish-green ragbag lichen. Deeper into the forest, the spruce give way to the other main components of the temperate rainforest. After the *Sturm und Drang* of the surf and rock, the forest is soft and embracing, and astonishingly quiet. Here the footing is trickier than on the shelf, with wet, exposed tree roots a significant and constant threat to one's balance.

The trail is boggy now, a sponge for all the mountain runoff. There are dozens of skunk cabbage, giving off the pungent odour that earned them their name. We settle into a pattern that will repeat itself for miles to come, the trail alternating between mud holes, gnarled roots, boardwalks, bridges, and ladders. At Thistle Creek (Trisle Creek, by some reckoning) there's a nice inland campsite and a lovely clear pool, but the coast is too much of a draw and we plough on. We hear Camper Creek before we see it from on high in the forest. A quick descent takes us to a cable car across the stream. We've hiked about five miles thus far today, and when we take off our packs at the cable car landing, we almost levitate, so light are we on our feet.

But this is no time to savour the feeling of weightlessness, because it's begun to rain hard. We clamber aboard the cable car and, hunched against the rain, haul ourselves and our packs to the other side. Camper Bay can be tricky to get to when the creek is running high, although it's worth the trip. The Natives called it *Qawshadt*, or "place where you get salmonberries." There's a good campsite at the creek mouth, and on a very low tide it's possible to hike the shelf to Sandstone Creek. But Dave and I are confronted with both a high creek and a rising tide, so we stick to the trail. That means a climb out of the ravine, and another two and a half miles of what the Sierra Club guidebook blithely calls "routine slogging." Actually, it is so wet here, so miserable, and we are getting so tired, that this stretch begs questions

FOLLOWING PAGE. *Among the giants: old-growth along the West Coast Trail.*

like: Why do people hike? How much farther is it? Boy, wouldn't a cold beer taste great right about now? In short, questions that have troubled existential philosophers for centuries, and still remain largely unanswered.

As we approach Sandstone Creek, Dave spots a trillium in flower. The trail is lined with ferns, the maidenheads unfurling their fiddlehead scrolls. False lily of the valley blanket whole swatches of the forest floor, and bunchberry, or dwarf dogwood, bloom along the trail's perimeter. The bridge is out at Sandstone Creek, so we shimmy across the slimy rock face above the falls. The creek mouth below the falls is a pretty spot but offers no campsite, so we decide to bivouac at Cullite Cove, now just a little more than a mile away. As we're bracing to climb away from Sandstone Creek, we encounter a lone hiker headed in the opposite direction, who claims to have hiked the trail every year for the past 15. Meeting other hikers is a mixed blessing on a trek like this. One of the principal reasons for even doing such a hike is to "get away," and after hours spent establishing a rhythm together, Dave and I find the presence of another hiker a mild intrusion. But then he's hiking alone, clearly not a great lover of company, so it's not as if he wants to bond any more than we do. And meeting him at least gives us a forewarning of what's to come. Getting to our destination, Cullite Cove, will be "interesting," he says. He mumbles something about ladders and, somewhat ominously, rope, and then waves us goodbye. Two nervy Steller's jays dart along the river canyon as we climb toward this particular day's manifest destiny.

After seven hours of hiking, at 5:00 p.m., cold, tired, and wet, we emerge from the cloying gloom of the forest to a wooden platform high above Cullite Creek. I count 136 steps straight down, but it's at least 80 fewer than we need to get to the creek. Several massive spruce have been downed by winter storms and have taken out the two bottom ladders. Actually, the whole cliffside has just peeled away, as if scalped, and a vile tangle of tree trunks, broken branches, mud, rock, and ladders lies in a sodden pile beneath our feet. We're standing now on a platform, suspended, as if on a cherry picker, about 50 feet above where we want to be. We slide around behind the ladder and begin a graceless, nervous slither across wet rock, bushwhacking

"False lily of the valley blanket whole swatches of the forest floor."

through prickly thickets of salmonberry, our bare hands stripping ferns as we work desperately to get a grip. Somehow we manage to half climb, half fall down to the creek's edge. I recall reading somewhere in the guidebook that the forest floor is "biologically diverse," and by now I've either seen it all about an inch from my straining face, or I'm wearing it. As we pick the detritus of the last 50 feet out of our hair and ears, we discover that we're standing in a grove of delicate, late-flowering pink fawn lilies. This delightful antidote to the last few minutes is, alas, short-lived.

It seems the same event that brought the ladders crashing down also dispatched another section of the cliff, blocking the trail down to the beach and our intended camp. So we wade the stream, boots and all at this point, and bushwhack down the opposite shore. The creek curves in a long loop, pooling behind the beach before cutting a narrow channel to the sea. We have to cross back to reach our camp and, exhausted now, we plunge in without a thought. Suddenly, what looked like a thigh-deep pool is up around our chests. Committed, we have no choice but to lurch forward, arms cocked back beneath our packs in a vain attempt to keep them out of the water. After a few seconds, gasping and shivering, we scramble to dry land and shake off the excess water like a couple of sodden dogs. Had we stopped to think we might have stripped, might even have hoisted our packs on high, might even have dropped them into plastic garbage bags we'd packed for just such an occasion. As it is, miraculously, most of our food and gear is relatively dry, and we quickly drop out of our wet clothes.

Dave lights a fire worthy of a funeral pyre, and we begin to thaw out. His camera gear got an unwelcome bath, but over the next few days most of it will revive. Right now, though, we're a little tense and a lot worn out. Dave reveals a previously unheralded treasure, which is a bottle of E. Guigal Côtes-du-Rhône, 1990, which, along with my Mediterranean Pasta Supreme, rounds the burrs off what was a wonderful day, with a rather glum ending. After a reassuring wink from the American lighthouse on Tatoosh Island, off Cape Flattery on the Olympic Peninsula, we collapse into the tent like deadfall timbers.

Pink fawn lily: a delightful, albeit short-lived antidote to a hard day on the trail.

D AY BREAKS SUNNY AND WARM, THE SKY CLOUDLESS. WE spend much of the morning drying out. A fog bank rolls in as I take time to explore the cove, which is scooped out of huge sandstone cliffs, maybe 100 feet high. Round grey rocks the size of cabbages are rolled around like buckshot by the surf. A story, apocryphal no doubt, has it that Cullite Cove derives its name from Kowshet, as it appeared on old charts, which referred to elk droppings on the beach. There is no evidence of anything having been near the beach overnight, however. Nor is there any evidence that this was once a place where Natives landed whales after dispatching them with harpoons, as they did all along the coast. A ship's officer named Fleurieu, venturing forth from *La Solide* in 1791, was highly impressed with the Nuu-chah-nulth's large canoes, from 30 to 35 feet in length and constructed with "intelligence and art." He was particularly taken with their fishing gear, specifically with the "furniture" they used for whaling. "The strong lance . . . is intended for striking the whale, when he presents himself on the surface of the water. . . . But the most difficult is not, undoubtedly, to deprive the monster of life; it remains for them to get possession of him: and it would never be believed,

The sea at work, insistently rewriting the shore.

27

A Nuu-chah-nulth canoe constructed with "intelligence and art." Etching by Frederic Remington, Harper's New Monthly Magazine, *December 1891.*

if we were not assured of the fact, that with skiffs so slight and ticklish, as canoes hollowed out of the trunk of a tree, a few men should succeed in dragging the space of four or five leagues an enormous mass, and contrive to run it on shore on a beach where they can cut it up: it cannot be believed that it was given to men, who are not sons of gods, to execute, with the sole help of their hands, these real labours of Hercules."

My morning is punctuated, rather more cleanly than Fleurieu's prose, with the discovery that the headlands are impassable at either side of Cullite Cove, and it's clear we're going to have to repeat at least part of the performance that got us here in order to get back out. We pack, but we're slow about it, as if delaying will some-how lessen the impact of what is to come. In fact, Dave and I do find a better way back across Cullite Creek. A huge deadfall spruce spans two-thirds of the stream, although the last 30 feet of it is submerged. I make a dummy run without my pack and discover we can cross without going deeper than mid-thigh. I do it again with my pack, legs wobbling under the weight, nervous about slipping and ending up wetter than before. In the end we both survive the crossing, if only to face an awful

20-minute bushwhack back upstream to the trail. My reward is that, once there, I get to lie on warm rocks in the riverbed while Dave spends 20 minutes photographing the pink fawn lilies we found the night before. From my low vantage point the sun on the stream as it slithers toward the sea makes it shimmer like mercury. Insects dance above its riffles, and a couple of sharp-eyed robins watch for anything that might constitute lunch. This is just the sort of interlude you don't get if you hike the trail too fast, and it's something that will lodge in your mind far longer than the sight of your boots clumping homeward.

We prepare to leave Cullite Creek, and discover that the ladders on the west side have survived a landslide similar to the torrent that took out the eastern ladders. They've survived, but barely. In fact, about 50 feet above us a long ladder has twisted in the middle in a wide sideways curve. Wrenched free from its anchors, it hangs in mid-air. Dave goes ahead and, right at the suspect spot, the timbers creak ominously. But the ladder holds for both of us and soon we're back on top, heading toward an extraordinary bog. Just at the boardwalk where the bog begins, I spy what looks like jellyfish in a puddle. Actually, they're frog eggs, the earliest hint of tadpoles suspended like freckles in clear aspic. An adult frog croaks, disgruntled at our intrusion, and we move on.

The boardwalk is weathered and covered in moss, and the wood is so waterlogged that it's hard to know what's moss and what's not. This tenuous, suspended walkway threads its way into a bog of stunted, tortured-looking trees, among them the occasional yew, shore pine, red cedar, and bunchberry. Most of the trees are dead, and those that are alive hang on grimly to a bed of spongy sphagnum moss. Yet, as starved and bereft as this place looks, the bog contains its own wonders. One of them is an insect-eating sundew plant, a delicate sign of life rising out of the almost apocalyptic landscape.

We descend from the bog to Logan Creek, whose mouth is wide and flat after the constraints of Cullite Cove. The Native name for Logan Creek is *Wiʔeːʔ* which translates as "negative beach" for some unexplained reason. There is good camping on the west side of the creek mouth at the beach, which is the most southerly sandy

FOLLOWING PAGE. *Boardwalk: slippery when wet.*

beach on the trail. For that reason it tends to attract more than its fair share of the ocean's *disjecta membra*: flotsam, and its constant companion, jetsam. With little effort one can spot all manner of junk along the tide line: old tires, wire cable, rope, a crab trap, buckets, a smashed cabin light, endless varieties of buoys in all colours. The truly fortunate might come across a glass buoy still intact, washed up all the way from Japan. I once found a refrigerator on the beach, and apparently most of the contents of a container of Nike shoes and boots once bobbed ashore near the Carmanah light-house. From Logan Creek it's theoretically possible to make it to Walbran Creek along the shelf, although the tide has to be lower than six feet and one has to be prepared to risk it all at the Adrenaline surge channel. This daunting chasm runs all the way to the cliff and can only be crossed when the sea is calm, the tide is low, and Adrenaline Creek is not running so high that its waterfall makes the surrounding rocks too slip-pery. Park officials warn against making this crossing, and since people have actually died in the attempt, it's a warning worth heeding. The alternative, our route for the day, is back on the trail, which the guidebook dryly describes as "slow and uninter-esting, but not difficult."

"Treasures" from the sea: a Japanese glass buoy after a long voyage.

32

Actually, crossing Logan Creek is great fun. There's a long, high suspension bridge, a wondrous bit of engineering that yields with an exhilarating bounce and sway as we cross it. After Cullite Creek, this crossing is a terrific luxury. Soon, though, we're slogging away at two miles of tangled roots, bog, and thick black gumbo that is deceptively deep. Sometimes knee-deep. The only thing more disgusting than sinking your whole foot into the mud is the sucking sound it makes when you retrieve it. We squelch through the muck and mire and speculate how this must compare with New Guinea's Kakoda Trail, knowing all along that our route is surely tame by comparison. At least there aren't leeches here. In stretches like this it is all too easy to simply watch one's boots and never pay any mind to the forest. So we pause for a while, hitching our packs onto dank, moss-covered stumps, steam rising from our overheated frames.

The forest is fecund, or "decadent," as an industrial forester would put it. Looking about us, here in the labyrinth, it's easy to understand why forests have exercised such a powerful force over human imagination down through the centuries. We see no faeries or forest demons darting around us, just a bulbous banana slug and animal tracks in the mud that I'm ready to embrace as those of a cougar, but which Dave assures me amount to nothing more exotic than a raccoon. Yet surely there are spirits here. I think of Tolkien, and Conrad, and Dante's *Inferno*, where

> *In the middle of our life's path*
> *I found myself in a dark forest,*
> *Where the straight way was lost.*

I think of the *Epic of Gilgamesh,* and of Vico's bestial giants, and of the Brothers Grimm, whose fairy tales captured so compellingly our species' mixture of enchantment and fear whenever we step into the wild heart of a forest. So lodged are those tales in the German psyche, it's no surprise that many Germans flock to British Columbia's dark and brooding rainforests. Germans actually consider forests the cradle of their race, and their own *Waldsterben,* or dying forest, makes them

appreciate all the more the rarity and value of what little forest we've had the sense to preserve in Canada.

Our bodies begin to cool, and it's time to step out of the realm of myth and back into the here and now. It isn't long before those "Why am I doing this?" questions begin to interpose themselves again, but today the answer arrives quickly in the form of Walbran Creek, or *Kaxi:ks,* or "big river." At the end of a short descent out of the woods, we're back on the coast, the creek racing toward the surf, gulls wheeling, a bracing offshore breeze blowing, brilliant sunshine pouring over us. A downed tree has swatted the cable car, rendering it completely unusable, so we wade the river at the mouth. With the exception of Cullite Creek and our near-total immersion there, I've been fastidious about keeping my boots as dry as possible. But at this point they're so gummed up with mud that I just plunge into the Walbran and actually get a good wash for my pains. On the west side of the creek we lie on warm rocks and take stock while two big eagles float overhead, trying to decide whether we represent a risk or a meal. In the end, they figure on neither.

The Walbran marks the start of the beach hiking that changes the whole tenor of the West Coast Trail for the next eighteen miles. That bracing breeze now borders on a gale. We suit up in our jackets and, wet feet notwithstanding, slip into a comfortable gait along the shelf, which quickly deposits us on a beach the colour and texture of ground pepper, the sand pleated along its edges by the wind. I'm soon reminded how hard it is, laden with a pack, to hike on sand. Half the effort of every step gets lost, and it's murder on the calf muscles. Where we can we stick to the shelf, making good time to the snap and crackle of tiny sea snails, while popweed explodes under our boots. The shelf is crenellated, and it's tricky work trying to walk in anything like a straight line. Eventually the incoming tide forces us off the shelf and we traipse heavily along the beach. The word *mule* comes to mind.

After the rigours of the previous day, we'd decided to make for Vancouver Point and call it quits today after just four miles. Somehow, though, we overshoot Vancouver Point and surprise ourselves when the Carmanah lighthouse hoves into view. In fact, we're nearing Bonilla Point, we've hiked six miles, and the wind is now

An exhilarating crossing: bridge over Logan Creek.

howling off the sea such that we can barely make headway. We pass by Kalide Creek, which puts us in the middle of the Pacheedaht's Cullite Indian Reserve 3. There was once a "big village" here, a safe landing for canoes and a place where Natives dried halibut and seaweed. Just along from here is Bonilla Point, which marks the dividing point between Pacheedaht territory and Ditidaht country. So we cross an ancient unmarked border and, in the lee of the trees near the mouth of Bonilla Creek, we camp. This time there's little of the purposeful determination that marked our first night out. Now our shoulders ache and our hips are sore and we hobble stiffly about our chores. Dave and I console ourselves with two packets of soup to get warm, followed by a rather ambitious Chili Mexicana and an even more outlandish Blueberry Cobbler (all freeze-dried, of course). The chili actually tastes something like the real thing. The cobbler? *Glutinous maximus.*

Dave, as is his habit, wanders off after dinner in anticipation of capturing the sunset. I make coffee and shuffle down to the shore, fingers bent around my cup for warmth. The scene is quite a spectacle, and for 15 or so minutes before the sun dips from view, it hangs in a distant bank of mist, which seems to cool the fire at its edges. Just for a moment or two the sun looks like a bright silver disk, a freshly minted coin. Then it regains its fiery glow, its colour, and slips behind the horizon. As it slides from view, waves dancing in the foreground fuel the illusion that the sun's heat has set the entire ocean aboil. Watching the disk disappear, I am suddenly struck with an uncanny feeling, almost like vertigo. I sense that I'm literally standing on the edge of our planet and that we're spinning adrift, tipping over and over as we barrel through the cosmos.

Shockingly Dave and I have no alcohol drink, but the sky is clear so we sit by the fire and drink in the stars. Tonight the spring constellations are like the delicate first blooms of the season. In August a fortunate few will witness the Perseid meteor shower, and be awestruck.

In August, a Perseid meteor shower over Bonilla Point.

M ORNING'S LIGHT HAS TO STRUGGLE AGAINST THE OCEAN fog, a process that mirrors what's happening inside our heads as we shake off a long, deep sleep. Eventually great shafts of sunlight burst through the treetops, fractured by the forest canopy as if in a kaleidoscope. The word *cathedral* gets bandied around a lot in reference to forests, and it is no accident. In the Germanic north the forests once housed a god, and in *Forests: The Shadow of Civilization,* Robert Pogue Harrison writes: "The Gothic cathedral visibly reproduces the ancient scenes of worship in its lofty interior, which rises vertically toward the sky and then curves into a vault from all sides, like so many tree crowns converging into a canopy overhead. Like breaks in the foliage, windows let in light from beyond the enclosure." And, indeed, at Bonilla Point, the light that filters through the treetops and the fog has an almost dusty quality against the gloom of the dark walls of the forest, reminiscent of the ethereal grandeur of the great Gothic cathedral in Seville. Looking the opposite way, we can see that the sea stacks at Bonilla Point are evocative, weather-beaten pinnacles. A lone tree clings obstinately to one. Another monolith looks like a stern-faced Native chief, a few tufts of grass clinging to the "face," as if the chief had shaved clumsily. The Natives called

Sunlight fractures the canopy: the word cathedral *springs to mind.*

39

these sea stacks ʔiʔi.weyl, or "one who follows behind his sweetheart," and it looks as if there will be hell to pay when the chief finally catches up with her.

This is an inspirational place, and we're in no hurry to leave. Two seals come into the creek mouth and do a little fishing. Two pairs of harlequin ducks bob in the water, and a colony of cormorants clusters on one of the sea stacks. A lone great blue heron is sequestered on a rock. The herring gulls make most of the noise, although, as at every other camp along the way, winter wrens and song sparrows contribute the harmonies. On the shore we find rocks containing fossilized tube worms and clam shells. A grove of sea palms is tugged at by the swirl of surf and tide, and on the beach there are tangles of bull kelp whose holdfasts finally surrendered to a greater force than their own grip. Just below the waterfall, where a mangled bridge pretends to cross Bonilla Creek, the forest has almost entirely subsumed the timbers from a wrecked boat. On the other side of the creek, right near the mouth, there is the wreck of a small logging boom boat. A tiny, solitary sandpiper perches nervously on the keel. On the rocks a flock of black turnstones chortles away. Red-beaked oyster catchers are too busy eating to notice much beyond the end of their snouts. They seem not to know, or care, that the morning fog has all but burned right off now. In the distance cargo ships head out toward where, Japan? Carrying what? Clear-grained yellow cedar, no doubt, and Canadian jobs forgone. Closer to shore a troller struggles through the swells, heading home. We decide to move on, but to go no farther than the glimmering crescent beach at Carmanah just around the corner. It takes almost no time to reestablish our camp up in the beach grass above the tide line. Nor does it take long to reacquaint ourselves with one of the real highlights of the entire trail.

In high summer Carmanah Beach is a mecca for a huge, seething flock of gulls that concentrates at the creek mouth. It's a big draw, too, for campers. It's a luscious scoop of sand, the western portion of which is a Native reserve. Of late, there has been a ramshackle settlement here – a couple of shacks, an extensive vegetable garden, a beachside cookhouse – that constitutes the headquarters of the "Independent State of Qwa-Ba-Diwa." The occupants' claim to statehood is probably best

An inspirational place: sea stacks at Bonilla Point.

explained by them, and they will offer a fulsome disquisition with little provocation. They also sell soft drinks and flapjacks with syrup; whether that enhances or detracts from the West Coast Trail's wilderness experience is a matter of personal taste. But with or without the presence of the Qwa-Ba-Diwa, the Carmanah has always been a rich lode for the diligent explorer.

In the rocks a careful search will reveal small seams of coal. Indeed the next notable creek to the west is named Coal Creek, site of an attempt in 1911 to mine coal under the auspices of the Carmanah Coal Company. There are, in fact, coal outcroppings from Bonilla Point clear to the Klanawa River, although mercifully none were ever exploited successfully. The name Carmanah resonates today

A mecca for gulls and people alike.

because of another attempt at exploitation, it, too, stillborn. In 1988, just a few short years ago, the Western Canada Wilderness Committee launched a spirited campaign to preserve the entire Carmanah Valley adjacent to the West Coast Trail. When you hike the trail, it's easy to take for granted the clear-running streams that sluice over rock and slice through sand to reach the sea. But don't take them for granted. The fact is, the West Coast Trail doesn't exist in isolation. The streams run out of valleys that have weathered numerous assaults, well out of sight of the shore. The coastal temperate rainforest derives from an amazing, self-replenishing cycle between land and sea, and so any ruin done to any part of it is an affront to the entire system. In the case of the Carmanah – and other places contiguous with the

trail, like Cullite, Logan, and Sandstone creeks, as well as the Walbran, the Klanawa, the Black River, and Michigan Creek – industry has sought to log heavily in the reaches above the trail.

In 1990 the Carmanah received a partial reprieve when the 10,000-acre Carmanah Pacific Provincial Park was established, preserving the lower part of the watershed where it connects with the trail. That same year the first marbled murrelet nest ever found in Canada was spied in the Walbran Valley, and in 1991 the Walbran became the focus of protests and logging blockades. Finally, in 1994, the entire Walbran Valley was spared from logging, as was the Upper Carmanah, which had been excluded from the original Carmanah park when it was set up in 1990. Other valleys that feed down to the trail weren't so lucky, which is especially so the closer you get to Bamfield. For example, the Klanawa River has been hit hard outside the park boundaries, according to Paul George of the Western Canada Wilderness Committee. "They have just devastated that area," says George. But at least the Carmanah and Walbran were spared.

In theory the expanded Carmanah Pacific *Provincial* Park has nothing to do with the Pacific Rim *National* Park, and the national park tries to discourage any connection between the two. The reason is simple: the West Coast Trail is a singular entity, and much of its charm lies in the fact that it can only be accessed from either end. Linking it to the Carmanah park in a sense pricks the bubble, diminishes the exclusivity. So hikers are urged to see the Carmanah separately, and it's worth the trip. The Carmanah watershed is a serene and embracing place, home to wonderful groves of Sitka spruce strung along a joyous watercourse. Chief among the Sitkas is the Carmanah Giant, at 312 feet the tallest tree in Canada and the tallest known Sitka spruce in the world. This behemoth became the poster child of the campaign to preserve the entire Carmanah, and clearly it struck a chord with the nation. So today Carmanah Creek runs clear, cleaving its way from the windward island mountains to the Pacific without industrial intervention.

Back at the shore, directly below the lighthouse at the far western end of Carmanah Beach, is a small stretch known locally as Swing Beach. In the rocks here

The Carmanah Giant: Canada's tallest known tree.

is a fossilized skull, thought to be that of some sort of ancient marine mammal, possibly a precursor to the sea otter. Indeed, at low tide there are veritable seams of fossils in this area. There are rock pools replete with bloodstar starfish, chitons, periwinkles, limpets, crabs, and bullheads. There are pink sea anenomes, whose sticky tendrils grab harmlessly, if disconcertingly, at a proferred finger. And there are sea urchins tucked into rock hollows that look like egg cartons, which protect the sea urchins from heavy swells. As we stumble from one revelation to another, Dave and I hear before we see about a dozen harbour seals concealed behind a high shelf of rock. They haven't spotted us yet, so we tiptoe up behind the rock and emerge just 20 feet from them, only a narrow channel of water separating us. Predictably, as soon as they get an eyeful of us, they bail off their perches, ungainly as they belly off the rocks, but slick as salesmen once they hit the water.

Jutting out of the rocks nearby are metal rods, remnants of the old gangway that used to lead up to the lighthouse. The light was established in 1891, and even though the concrete tower isn't an original, this sturdy bastion is worth a look, if only for

Starfish and sea anenomes: a sticky place for a finger.

Fruits of an abundant shoreline: limpets and a bloodstar starfish.

the views from the point. Close at hand is a sea lion haul-out rock, carpeted with a velvety mass of Steller's and California sea lions. From the Carmanah lighthouse, it's possible to see the Pachena lighthouse, which is about as far again as we've already hiked. At Carmanah we've come 20 miles of the 47. After a day of relative indolence, the realization that we've still so far to go means we plan to make tracks the following morning.

FOLLOWING PAGE. *A velvety mass of sea lions near Carmanah Point: snobs every one of them.*

FROM CARMANAH WEST THE TRAIL BEGINS TO INTERSECT WITH the richest elements of human settlement along this stretch of the Pacific shore. All along the coast now – sometimes obvious, most often not – are signs of lost generations of Native and European settlers. Agate Beach was a favoured potlatch place, and even today at least one Native elder can be seen here in the form of a rock outcrop known as Indian Head, which aptly describes what the rock looks like when viewed in profile. Right opposite, on the beach, Dave discovers a coconut. Nonplussed, we scour the tree line above us to ensure that global warming hasn't somehow spawned a grove of palm trees, and conclude instead that this is just another odd bit of flotsam. A check of its innards confirms that it's come a long way. Farther along from here are the jaunty natural breakwater of the Bay of the Cribs, and the "squeaking" or "whistling" sands, so-called for the sound made by walking on them. Here we see another river otter before delving back into the forest and once more picking up the trail.

It's a cloudy day – the perfect temperature for hiking. At either side of the trail cattails grow in profusion and we see but don't sample numerous miner's lettuce. The trail works along the cliff after a steep climb from the Cribs, working back to the

Calm before the storm: Carmanah Point lighthouse is a beacon to mariners plying the Strait of Juan de Fuca.

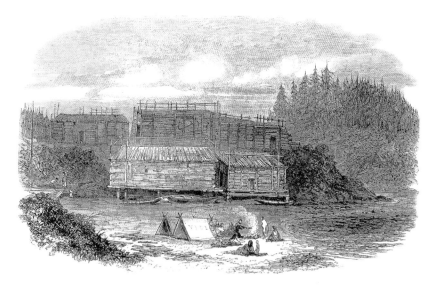

This drawing of Native longhouses at Whyac in 1864 was published in the London Illustrated News *in 1866.* ROYAL BRITISH COLUMBIA MUSEUM

beach around Dare Point, which is the approximate halfway point for the entire trail and a welcome landmark. There is more frequent beach access here than at the bottom end of the trail, more campsites but often less water. The trail to the Cheewhat River – a sluggish tidal stream known to the Indians as the "river of urine" for its off colour and taste – goes over old sand dunes that are forested now. Ironically the closer we come to what were traditionally the most settled areas of the trail, the less welcome we are to explore in any detail. It is possible to glimpse the remains of some old buildings in and around Clo-oose, which has by turns been a Native settlement, home to the first white homesteaders and missionaries out here, and now a Native reserve. There was even a post office here until the 1960s, and for decades this was the main supply point along this coast: the very name Clo-oose means "safe landing" in the Nitinat language. Today the Ditidaht band requires that hikers remain on the trail and not camp on reserve lands, and only the most ignorant fail to comply with their wishes. The trail climbs from Clo-oose to a cliff, but then bypasses the ancient village of Whyac, which is Nitinat for "lookout." This is said to be one of the oldest villages on the West Coast of all North America, home to Natives drawn to the salmon runs in the narrows and to the migrating grey whales that pass right by here. Again the Ditidaht ask that people stay off the side trails to Whyac.

Quite how the Ditidaht came to hold sway over this region of the trail in the first place is open to debate, although it is believed they, the Ohiaht, and the Pacheedaht were once a single people living together at a place called *Diitiida,* or what we now know as Jordan River. (You pass through Jordan River on the drive from Victoria to Port Renfrew.) One story is that *Diitiida* became overcrowded, and the Ditidaht travelled along the West Coast until they reached the entrance to Nitinat Lake; the Ohiaht migrated farther up the coast to where Bamfield now stands. Other accounts relate to "the Flood" when "the salt water rose over the land and covered everything." When the waters subsided, the Ditidaht settled near the mouth of the Nitinat Narrows at a place called *Waayaaʔak̓,* or Whyac. The Ditidaht themselves "came to dominate the region," according to an ethnographic history of the coast. There was, of course, no trail at this point. When Nuu-chah-nulth people wanted to roam beyond their villages, they did so in their cedar canoes.

In the 18th century Duffin and Fleurieu recorded some of the earliest contact with the Ditidaht, or as they were often known, the Nitinaht. But, as mentioned earlier, this stretch of the coast was less hospitable than Nootka and Clayoquot

The old Ditidaht village of Carmanah at the turn of the century.

sounds, so development occurred slowly. But in the 19th century it did happen, stemming largely from the diligent work of William Banfield, who was appointed government agent in 1859 by Governor James Douglas. Banfield centred his operations near what is now Bamfield, and he peppered the governor with reports of the area and how it might be exploited. (Bamfield was supposed to be named after Banfield, but his name was misspelled when the post office was established there, and the misprint stuck.) A major exploration was mounted by Captain Robert Brown, whose Vancouver Island Exploring Expedition came down the Nitinat River in the summer of 1864, encountering numerous salmon weirs and, on Nitinat Lake, passing abandoned villages until reaching "Wye-yack" (Whyac) at the mouth of the narrows. Brown wrote: "The Nitinats were at one time a very powerful tribe, the terror of the coast but they have shared in the universal decay, and do not number 400 fighting men – They are still great bullies..." Hiring a war canoe with three pilots, Brown headed down the coast, journeying past "Kloos" (Clo-oose), "Quamadooa" (Carmanah), and on to Port San Juan, where he found the aforementioned "thinned" tribe of Pacheedaht people.

In 1871 British Columbia joined the Confederation of Canada. Jurisdiction over Native affairs fell to the Dominion government, and the next year Dr. I. W. Powell became the new province's first Indian commissioner. He toured Barkley Sound aboard HMS *Boxer* in 1873, and the following year instructed George Blenkinsop to live among the Indians there "for the purpose of acquiring an intimate knowledge of their wishes in regard to lands to be hereafter reserved for them..." In 1882 negotiations began with Natives on the West Coast. Reserves were defined and surveyed over the course of the ensuing decade (and later pruned further by the McKenna-McBride commission in 1913-16), and the nomadic patterns of the Nuu-chah-nulth were quickly and effectively constrained. Others had designs on their lands and resources. Indeed the plundering of all British Columbia had begun in earnest.

Although far-flung and difficult to service, the area around Nitinat Lake attracted some hardy European settlers. In 1890 William H. Grove became the first of several "preemptors" who acquired land in the area. Grove built a store at Clo-oose and

Hikers perched over a powerful surf. Once, powerful tribes were the terror of this coast.

54

traded with Ditidaht sealing crews who worked on ships in the North Pacific and came home with cash wages, looking for a place to spend them. Grove's property was reduced to an acre of land when the Native reserve was laid out, so he bought large properties up the Cheewat River in 1892 and ran cattle there. Grove later decided to go to Australia and, upon meeting a Scotsman in Victoria, convinced him to go to Clo-oose to look after Grove's interests. David Logan moved to Clo-oose in 1894, arriving aboard the steamship *Maude*. Reverend Stone, a Methodist, established a mission at Clo-oose that same year to minister to the Ditidaht. (Logan, in addition to his rather Pyrrhic pursuit of a decent living as a farmer and trader, was to become a line repairman on the telegraph line.)

Clo-oose achieved a measure of equilibrium over the years as a trading post, fishing outpost, service centre for the telegraph line, and home to both Natives and Europeans. It remained the principal "safe landing" along the coast, such that even in 1910 when the Carmanah Coal Company attempted to extract coal from seams along the coast, it landed its equipment at Clo-oose. As mentioned earlier, nothing ever came of the coal venture, and not much came of the West Coast Development Company, either. This was a bold gamble, just before the outbreak of World War I, to turn the area around the mouth of the Nitinat into an English-style beach resort. The site was actually called Clovelly after the bucolic seaside community in North Devon. Speculators off-loaded plenty of lots, and there were schemes for a golf course, hotel, and mineral spas, as well as a boardwalk and an ocean pier. Plans were also made for a coast road, a rail line into the head of Nitinat Lake, and ships ferrying people and supplies up and down the lake. In the end a log clubhouse and dining hall known as the Bungalow Inn was built, and a tent village that could accommodate about 100 people sprung up as a prelude to building cabins. The whole enterprise came to nought, though, with the onset of the war.

Toward the end of the war the Lummi Bay Packing Company set up shop inside the narrows at a place that's come to be known as Cannery Bay. The cannery quickly became one of the biggest producing plants on Vancouver Island, in part because the narrows and Nitinat Lake were grossly overfished. In its heyday the cannery employed many Natives, but by the mid-1920s the fishery was on the wane and the canning plant finally shut down for good. When the cannery died, so did any prospects for a prosperous, permanent settlement, and the population dwindled steadily. The death knell for the community came in the 1950s when the coastal steamer *Maquinna* was withdrawn from service to Clo-oose. A postal service was maintained until 1963, but Clo-oose was all but abandoned soon after and the coast's harsh elements quickly consumed most of the buildings. Not that much has changed since.

As we leave Clo-oose, Dave and I pass a viewpoint where the anchor of the barkentine *Skagit* can be spied on the shelf below. It was wrecked here in 1906, and it's easy to see why. From this point on the trail's raison d'être becomes more and more evident, because from here to the end of the hike is a stretch of coast that has claimed a heavy toll in ships and lives lost. But the essence of the shipwrecked mariner's trail lies on the other side of the Nitinat Narrows, and we hasten toward the great psychological hurdle it represents.

The trail takes us away from the outer coast, away from Whyac and inland toward a dock inside the narrows. Here patience and $5 a head gets us a boat ride

Bottleneck at the not-so-narrow Nitinat Narrows: a place to rest up and trade intelligence about what's in store.

Foxglove: one of the many beauties of the forest "wrapped in a seamless blanket of moisture."

on the Native ferry service to the other side of the narrows through which a turbulent guzzle of water flushes with alarming force. Other than getting onto the trail at Port Renfrew, this is the only point where one has to rely on anything but boots and stamina, and it's always a relief to flag down Carl Edgar, Jr., or his brother Terry, who whip hikers across the narrows by boat. This is also home to a dock where a rare bit of social intercourse takes place between hiking parties. Most people, respecting the desire of others to have as private an experience as possible, stagger their departure from camp each morning so as not to be hiking right on a stranger's heels. But at either side of the Nitinat an unavoidable bottleneck occurs, and if Carl and Terry are having any luck with their crab traps, quite a gathering of hikers can end up waiting for a lift. It's a great chance to share vital intelligence about the state of the trail in either direction. If the wait is a long one, invariably someone will suggest swimming the narrows or cobbling together a makeshift raft to get across. Some have even gone and done it, unaware of the immensity of Nitinat Lake or of the great drama around the corner where the lake's waters run smack into the incoming sea. Fishermen routinely capsize their boats on the tricky bar, and some aren't lucky enough to survive the experience. Hikers should keep their boots on. The ferry will come in good time.

We are well over halfway through the hike when we cross the narrows, 27 miles down and 20 to go. We gird for another climb to the clifftops on the western side, but our pleasure at making the crossing is tempered by the rather intemperate turn of the weather. Our intention had been to camp on the first beach after the narrows, but beautiful as it is, it promises nothing like the shelter we know of a little more than a mile away. So we take a bit more trail in stride and, with Hole-in-the-Wall visible in the distance at Tsusiat Point, repair to the woods and a roomy cave. Other tents are huddled against Tsusiat Point, but we don't even bother with a fly on our tent as we smugly set up shop while a curtain of rain closes just a few feet away. Dave and I set a modest fire and pass a luxuriously dry night tucked in by the Earth, knowing that outside our hollow the forest is wrapped in a seamless blanket of moisture.

FOLLOWING PAGE. *A commodious cave and a comfortable place to set up camp.*

HERE IS NO LETUP THE NEXT MORNING, AND THERE'S AN exponential disinclination on our part to move far in the downpour. We decide instead to make a few short trips free of the burden of our packs, and head first to Hole-in-the-Wall, exactly halfway between the Carmanah and Pachena lighthouses. On the beach we find what surely are cougar tracks in the sand and are strangely proud to have graduated from raccoon prints. Just offshore an exposed shelf is home to a couple of dozen seals. At this point in the trip such a sight could be considered routine, but frankly it's such a privilege to view them in the wild that we spend half an hour standing in the rain watching them do what they do, which appears to be nothing. We slip along the beach to Hole-in-the-Wall and race through it between the waves, coming in from two sides. Atop the arch, as if on the prow of a boat, we're treated to a superb 270-degree view as the weather lifts a little. Grey clouds sit like a steel lid over the swirling soup of the sea and, before they descend again, we decide to double back toward the Nitinat Narrows and explore the beaches along the way.

Forced back onto the trail at Tsuquadra Point, I see a bear paw print clearly stamped in the mud. Here again the Ditidaht band has closed access to its

Hole-in-the-Wall: a lookout and a place to race the waves at low tide.

Giant catacombs: now off-limits, and none the worse for it.

Tsuquadra Reserve, lands that "contain cultural and natural resources of great significance to the Ditidaht people." It is a federal offence to trespass, says the sign, and while we stand reading about how the area is patrolled by Ditidaht guardians and park wardens, a flock of brant geese honks raucously overhead, as if warning us to put aside any thoughts of disobeying the signs. Previous generations of hikers have caused the Natives to be wary, and in the end to ban them altogether from this area, in part because of the damage done to traditional buildings on the reserve. The ancient village here came to a sorry end with the smallpox epidemic at the turn of the century, and it is in this area that the Natives buried their dead, sitting up in open boxes, in sacred burial caves. Before a thoughtless few profaned the area and offended Native traditions it was possible to see faint signs of a longhouse here, as well as some of the coast's most spectacular sea caves aligned in a network of giant granite catacombs. They are off-limits now, but surely no less spectacular for the fact that one can no longer invade them.

The lid of clouds slams down once more on the water in the guise of a stinging rain squall. We head back in the direction of our rather commodious cave and await the late-afternoon low tide. I amble off down to look for what, according to the map, will be a ship's anchor visible among the rocks. I don't find any trace of it, but instead discover thickets of mussels colonizing every corner and crevice. So, my back set against the storm, I buckle down alongside a half-dozen oyster catchers and harvest a feed of shellfish. Parks Canada warns against the risk of PSP (paralytic shellfish poisoning), which is no joke. Then again, that needs to be weighed against the risk of eating another package of the MPS (Maritime Pasta Supreme) with nothing to accompany it. Caught between the devil and the deep blue, we cook the blighters, which turn bright orange after a turn in the pot and taste exquisite.

After days of food from packets, we flex some mussels . . . and survive.

MORNING BRINGS REASSURING NEWS THAT EACH OF US HAS feelings in our extremities, that the mussels wished us no ill. There is, however, no evidence that the weather will improve so we set our sights on hiking most of the way to Pachena Point in the rain: about 11 miles. The best comes first: Tsusiat Falls. With their trademark lack of linguistic irony, the Native word Tsusiat means "where the water runs down always," which indeed it does. Legend has it that the Natives used to build magnificent oceangoing canoes beside Tsusiat Lake and bring them downriver to the falls, where they lowered them over the precipice using ropes made from cedar withes. That would have been no mean feat, since the falls are enough of a landmark to be visible from the sea and used as a reference point for local shipping. They are also a great draw for hikers doing the entire West Coast Trail, or campers who hike in from Bamfield just to see the point where this alluring veil of water drops four stories to the beach and thence to the ocean. Popularity has its hazards, and the falls are invariably crowded, which can make for a great social scene if you're in the mood and a dreary reminder of the press of civilization if you're not.

The first time I ever hiked the trail I gave the entire trek a total of just five and

Tsusiat Falls: "where the water runs down always."

FOLLOWING PAGE. *By the light of the silvery moon: Lord Tennyson's campsite.*

67

a half days, which meant that by the time I got to Tsusiat Falls I was in such a rush to get to Bamfield and not miss my ride out on the MV *Lady Rose* that I never actually got to the falls. I merely crossed the river above them and hiked on. That's a sin right up there on a par with going to Rome for the first time and skipping the Sistine Chapel, and it's not a mistake I've repeated.

There are days on the West Coast, rare but spectacular days when the sun is hot and if you blinked, you'd swear you were in the South Pacific. There are days, languorous days, when hiking any farther than the water's edge seems like a peculiar folly. When such a day arrives, there's no better place to be than at the falls. And for those who have hiked all day in the heat, there's the singular pleasure of immersion under the healing waters of the Tsusiat. Of all the places along the trail it is surely the best designed for sloth. People, purists probably, have been known to leave behind wine in order to make room in their pack for a book to read along the way. If anywhere, this is the place to do nothing but sunbathe, swim, beachcomb and, if one is so moved, read. For compactness I rely on a 1925 edition of *The Poems of Alfred, Lord Tennyson,* and his irresistible *The Lotos-Eaters,* which I'm sure he must have penned while resting at Tsusiat Falls:

> All round the coast the languid air did swoon,
> Breathing like one that hath a weary dream.
> Full-faced above the valley stood the moon;
> And like a downward smoke, the slender stream
> Along the cliff to fall and pause and fall did seem.

But on this cold day the falls offer none but brief visual relief, while a hard rain falls over an ocean turned dull green, cold like slate. There is to be no surcease, and thus I conjure up more Tennyson:

> Why are we weigh'd upon with heaviness,
> And utterly consumed with sharp distress,
> While all things else have rest from weariness?

Suspended and animated: working the cable car across the Klanawa River.

"Indeed, Dave," I say, "'why should we toil alone,' and among other things, 'make perpetual moan?'" But Dave's not listening. He's already halfway up the ladder away from the falls, and we're a long way from Pachena Point.

We hike fast along the inland boardwalk, or as fast as possible on something that cambers alarmingly at times, collapses altogether at others, and all the while is slipperier than a toad's chin. On a couple of occasions we both slide off into the mud, and as often as not we hike alongside the boardwalk, not bothering to invite the inevitable. The trail skirts a high cliff all the way to the Klanawa River, but while we're high above the ocean now, we're not immune to its effect. A big surf is running and the waves are hitting the shore so hard that at one point, the entire cliff seems to shake. In fact, this is just the air vibrating – or so it seems, until we round a corner and find that a whole chunk of the cliff has slumped several feet. This is no place to take in the view, and we tread carefully. Soon we're suspended high over the Klanawa, working hand over hand at what will be our last cable car trip of the journey. We regain the beach and, for a while, take a breather under the overturned wreckage of a huge barge.

From this point on it's hard not to be slightly spooked by the history of this trail, and by the extent of the human suffering that has taken place here over the years. West of the Klanawa are the Valencia Bluffs, so named for the ship that went aground here in 1906 with tragic results. Along this stretch 126 people perished in a wretched mishap, many of them making it to shore alive, only to die of exposure because there was no decent route out. There is no sign of any wreckage from the *Valencia*, but especially on a windswept and miserable day like this, it takes little imagination to conjure up the carnage that must have visited this place back when the century was young. However, the *Valencia* was hardly the first ship to run afoul of this coast, just the most notorious.

As far back as 1786, a British pelagic sealing expedition lost two ships and 100 men somewhere off Vancouver Island's southern coast. The terrible swells and the unyielding coastline doubtless swallowed many other ventures in the ensuing years, their fates unrecorded. The first known wreck along the coast was the *William*,

Wrecked barge: a headstone in the "Graveyard of the Pacific."

which went ashore east of Pachena Point on New Year's Day, 1854. The captain and the cook were lost, and local Natives sheltered 14 survivors before rowing them down the coast to Sooke. By 1857 the Americans had installed a lighthouse at Tatoosh, off Cape Flattery. But despite being urged to install a complementary lighthouse at Bonilla Point, thereby framing the entrance of the strait for all to see, the British Admiralty was unmoved and dumped the request back in Canada's lap. It wasn't until 1872 that the Canadian government steamer *Sir James Douglas* set out from Victoria to survey a site for a lighthouse near Barkley Sound, which was being promoted at the time as a major port. That expedition failed, but the next year HMS *Tenedos* landed on a peninsula and cleared it to make way for a lighthouse at Cape Beale. "All equipment, including seven tons of lantern and machinery, made their way to the cleared station on the backs of local Indians," writes Donald Graham in *Keepers of the Light.* (No doubt unbeknown to the lighthouse builders was the fact that a major landmark at Cape Beale is "execution rock," from which the Natives once hurled their captives to death.) At Cape Beale, then, the entrance to Barkley Sound was duly marked, but still there was no Canadian beacon to guide ships into the Strait of Juan de Fuca.

A rapidly expanding traffic was plying the Strait of Juan de Fuca, bound for the booming "emporium" of Victoria Harbour, and the lesser harbours of Vancouver and Nanaimo. But this movement up and down the coast came at a considerable cost to the conquerors. In 1887 the British Columbia legislature demanded that Ottawa respond to "the great and urgent importance of having a lifesaving station established on the West Coast of Vancouver Island," an area the lieutenant governor noted was "entirely destitute of lifesaving appliances." Colonel W. P. Anderson, chairman of the Dominion Lighthouse Board, balked at the cost of putting lifeboats on the coast, "at least until the danger becomes more urgent or the white population denser." In any event, Anderson said, the Natives were "wonderfully expert" at plucking people out of the surf with their canoes. Anderson also said a proposed new lighthouse at Bonilla Point and a telegraph line between Victoria and Cape Beale would "decrease the dangers on that rugged coast." So, in 1887, fully 40 years since a Bonilla Point lighthouse had first been suggested to the Admiralty, and with hundreds of people having perished for lack of good bearings, Ottawa finally acted. It wasn't loss of life, but the loss of two days' sailing by the SS *Port Augusta* – stuck in fog and wasting money – that prompted construction of a lighthouse at Bonilla Point. Except no lighthouse was ever actually built at Bonilla Point, since the construction crew off-loaded its supplies in thick fog and, when the fog cleared, found itself at Carmanah Point. That's where the lighthouse still stands today after opening for business in 1891. Meanwhile, work had begun in 1888-89 to survey and build the telegraph line between Cape Beale and Victoria.

One of the principal functions of the telegraph line was to assist in rescue operations, assuming, of course, the telegraph functioned. More often than not it didn't. Writes Donald Graham: "Although linemen were nominally assigned to patrol each section weekly – checking for fallen wires, short circuits, or other interruptions – they often gave their patrols short shrift, viewing them as something to attend to after checking their cattle and traps. Even when windfalls were discovered, the sheer

An abandoned lineman's cabin: often the linemen gave their patrols short shrift,
promising more security than they could deliver.

labor involved in cutting through virgin coastal timber, up to ten feet thick, with an ax and Swede saw kept the line mute for days, even weeks." What had been established as a lifesaving network was, in fact, a poorly maintained and blithely underfunded link that promised more security than it delivered. W. P. Daykin, keeper of the Carmanah lighthouse, made repeated, scornful references to the failure of the line in his daily journal, but demands that the government improve the service went unheeded at the turn of the century. Ottawa was "charting a course between cruelty and cost while ships and men went down all round, leaving the wreckage of hulls and humans behind," writes Graham.

One of the most notorious wrecks was that of the *Janet Cowan,* which broke up off Pachena Bay on New Year's Eve, 1895. The surviving crew members were marooned on shore in deep snow for two weeks, starving and completely at a loss as to their whereabouts. The captain died after five days and, as others succumbed, the fittest survivors struck out north and south and were eventually rescued. Their tribulations were electrifying news to readers of the Victoria *Colonist;* in fact, the sorry plight of dozens of wrecked ships and crews was constant fodder for the newspapers, as well as a growing source of public concern. (By 1910 the *Colonist* tallied "700 lives and millions of dollars" lost along the coast.) But as dramatic as each account was, none so captured the public's imagination – or produced such widespread outrage – as the wreck of the *Valencia.*

Keepers of the Light gives a chilling account of what happened to the 154 people who were borne out of San Francisco on January 20, 1906. The Pacific Coast Line passenger ship was bound for Victoria but quickly became engulfed in fog. It groped north toward a grisly fate a few miles north and west of the Carmanah lighthouse, barely 300 yards away from where the *Janet Cowan* had succumbed 10 years earlier. The wreck of the *Valencia* was to surpass all but the sinking of the *Titanic* "in terms of sheer horror," Graham writes. "Yet there was a certain grim dignity in the latter's fate. None of that for the *Valencia,* whose crew and passengers were virtually tortured to death in a manner which sent a shock wave of revulsion around the world."

The ill-fated Valencia *surpassed all but the* Titanic *"in terms of sheer horror" when it ran aground in an unspeakable storm in January 1906.*

Like so many before him, the ship's captain misjudged his position, desperately seeking the Strait of Juan de Fuca and instead finding himself bearing down on the jagged West Coast shore. The *Valencia's* steel hull was pierced and the ship began to take on water. Rather than sink in deep water, the captain deliberately ran his vessel toward the rocks, where it jammed fast on a pinnacle about 30 yards offshore. There, it settled in to be pummelled by a relentless procession of huge, cold grey waves. Passengers were tossed overboard almost immediately. Women and children were lashed to rigging out of reach of the sea. "It was a pitiful sight to see frail women, wearing only night dresses, with bare feet on the frozen ratlines, trying to shield children in their arms from the icy wind and rain," wrote freight clerk Frank Lehm. Daybreak brought a grisly spectacle. "Bodies hung suspended from the rigging like flies in a web. Once rigor mortis had run its course they loosened their hold and tumbled into the water or onto the deck with a flaccid thud. More corpses drifted between ship and shore, scoured of flesh and features as if by a giant cheese grater," Graham writes. One lifeboat finally made it ashore and its crew soon found the telegraph trail, made it to a lineman's cabin, and cabled Cape Beale. Another vile night passed as rescuers struggled along the trail and ships sailed from Victoria to lend assistance.

After several failed attempts, the *Valencia* did finally get a lifeboat off the next day and its small crew was rescued by the *City of Topeka*. Another life raft was swept up toward Barkley Sound, and three survived. In all, though, 117 perished. Not a single woman or child survived, and with reporters on hand from the *New York Times* and elsewhere in the United States, the inadequacies of Canada's coastal rescue apparatus were laid bare to an incensed public. The embarrassment of commissions of inquiry in the United States and at home miraculously prompted Ottawa to find funds for a new lighthouse at Pachena Point, and to commit to a complete upgrade of the West Coast Trail from Port San Juan all the way to Cape Beale. Finally the Graveyard of the Pacific, as the area had come to be known, had so many corpses in it that the stench reached even Canada's capital.

Today there is nothing to show for the *Valencia,* although wreckage of the *Janet Cowan* can still be seen in a surge channel at the mouth of Billy Goat Creek at low

Billy Goat Creek: from the sea the falls look like a goat's beard.

tide. But neither Dave nor I are in the mood for much rock hopping along this sombre shore. In the sandstone Dave does spy two fossilized starfish, while I spot a dark scribble in the distant sky that eventually straightens out into a single file of brant geese flying overhead. I count 82. As we turn to regain the trail at Trestle Creek, two Australians emerge from the bush, headed to Tsusiat Falls for the night. "Just like southwestern Tasmania," they say rather too cheerfully, considering just how miserable this place is, both historically and meteorologically. We exchange news of the state of the trail in either direction, and they seem appropriately impressed at our tales from the bottom end of cliffs scaled and rivers forded. Certainly, by this time, we must look the part – muddied, slightly bloodied, stubbled, and no doubt a little on the ripe side. We clump off in the direction of Billy Goat Creek, so named for its waterfall that, viewed from the sea, appears like a goat's beard. I use the word *clump* advisedly, because by this point in the day we are wet through, our boots especially. Each foot feels as if it's stuck in a pot of cold porridge.

After Billy Goat Creek, we cross Tscowis Creek, which fairly gouges its way to the ocean through a violent and contorted gorge underfoot. The word *Tscowis* reportedly means "steep place – bluffs" in the Ditidaht tongue. We are too wet to bother with the cable car over the Darling River and just wade onward. On a more convivial day we'd be tempted by hidden falls just upstream on the Darling that most hikers never realize are there. Instead we make for Michigan Creek. Here at low tide, wreckage from the *Michigan,* which went down in 1893, can be found. Not by us, however, since at this point we're wrecked enough by our day's work and don't care to speculate on someone else's misery. Michigan Creek is the last good campsite before the trail ends, so it's where our day ends. We have seven miles left, so we can pack our sodden clothes into spare plastic bags, safe in the knowledge that we're just one last change of clothes away from hot running water.

Camping near the Darling River: forest, sea, tranquillity.

THE PACHENA LIGHTHOUSE'S FOGHORN SOUNDS ON AND OFF during the night, but after a predictably glum start, the morning brightens. The trail from here is a cakewalk; in fact, it used to be a road. In 1907, as part of the improvements hastened by the fate of the *Valencia,* a 12-foot-wide road was begun between Bamfield and Pachena Point, where the light station was built the same year. Building the road was an elaborate, largely useless exercise: it had been designed for horse-drawn rescue equipment that wasn't required. For all the bridges and culverts, for all the engineering that went into the road, it was constantly besieged by the elements, falling timbers knocking out what the raging waters hadn't already washed away. The road was too ambitious for the occasional needs of lifesavers, yet it never extended far enough, for instance to the Nitinat Narrows, to become a link to the burgeoning economic development there. But it did make for easy access to the new light station.

Today it makes for an easy stroll, certainly for a couple of trail-hardened hikers who have a week's exercise under their belts and who have gnawed through most of their rations. So Dave and I take time out after a bit more than a mile and stop in at Pachena Point. I'm tempted to search out *Chuʔdak̲suus,* which apparently

The photographer at work: self-portrait without shame.

83

After the first six miles from Bamfield, "welcome" to Pachena Point. Viewed from the other side, a welcome sign that the end is nigh.

translates as "vulva-mouth beach" and is said to be right near the point. I'm not quite sure what it is I intend to do when I get there but, as it is, I don't see any side trails and soon we're at the Pachena lighthouse instead. Gwen Fraser, wife of the principal lightkeeper, Doug Fraser, has handpainted Welcome on signs in 35 languages at the entrance to the lighthouse compound. Hikers starting at the Bamfield end have just walked their first six miles when they come to these signs and may little appreciate how welcome a sight they are to hikers like us, who now have the 41 hardest miles safely behind us.

The Pachena Point lighthouse is an eight-sided classic, the last original wooden light tower on the West Coast of Canada. Before that, it and Victoria were the first marine radio stations on the West Coast. The light was first lit, as close as Doug Fraser can reckon, on May 8, 1908. The dioptric lens, a first-order classical Fresnel lens of glass embedded in brass – 10 feet tall and eight feet across, afloat in a 900-pound mercury bath – was brought around Cape Horn in 1907 and pieced together on the point. It's an engineering masterpiece, and its 1,000-watt bulb, magnified,

Pachena Point lighthouse: the class of the field.

puts out four million candlepower. A beacon if ever there was one, it can be seen from the Olympic Peninsula in the United States.

The year after the Pachena lighthouse was lit, the grounding of the four-masted *Soquel* put to the test the new "lifesaving trail" and the various communications links that were finally in place. Almost everyone made it off the *Soquel* alive. The system worked... at least to a degree. In the 1920s the steamer *Alaskan* went down with all hands between Pachena Point and Cape Beale. Patrols on the trail were beefed up. Gradually, though, technology overtook what was, after all, a remarkably crude communications network. The telegraph gave way to a radio telephone and, after World War II, further advances in communications meant the trail was fast becoming redundant. In 1954 the Department of Transport abandoned the trail, although the telephone company maintained the section west of Carmanah until 1964 when all attempts to keep the trail open were given up. At the same time Coast Guard helicopters began bringing in the mail, the Clo-oose post office was closed, and the last coastal steamer to run supplies into that community, the *Tahsis Prince,*

Where the forest meets the sea: hiking along the fault line of the West Coast Trail.

made its final voyage to the area. The salal quickly began to reclaim the trail and, if not for the outdoor recreation boom and some farsighted conservationists, it would have disappeared forever… or at least until it was exhumed at the edge of a clearcut.

Just as Dave and I prepare to leave Pachena Point, we see a grey whale breach almost literally at our feet as it heads up the coast. We begin to migrate in the same direction and glimpse our last sea lion colony at a place called Flat Rocks, just as the trail hoves northward for the canter along the homestretch to Pachena Bay and the trail's end. From Pachena Point onward, we're in Ohiaht territory. We lope easily over the last six miles of the trail, cheerfully acknowledging the groups of neophytes as they come bundling along on their first day, spry and astonishingly clean. There is little useful access to the beach along this stretch and, in any case, we have the scent of home in our nostrils. Soon after crossing Clonard Creek, the hike is over. It ends in a clearing where a Christian camp once stood, and where Parks Canada now maintains an A-frame cabin. Ingress and egress.

Short side trails off the clearing lead to Pachena Beach, most of which is embraced by the Ohiaht's main reserve. The *Ho:ʔiʔatḥ* roamed all over these parts once in constant competition for their territory, battling other Nuu-chah-nulth bands, in particular the Uchucklesaht and the Ucluelet. These were reportedly brutal affairs, often fought over whale hunting rights. During the "Long War in Barkley Sound," a Ucluelet war party killed a young Ohiaht chief. The fighting lasted 10 years, and in some cases young girls were used as currency to pay neighbouring bands to attack the Ucluelet people. "The warring tribes eventually made peace by the exchange of women," according to one account. The other defining event in the history of the Ohiaht was an earthquake. The people of *Ch'ibataqsł*, or Cape Beale, are said to have taken refuge in a cave where they were trapped by a landslide. The people of *ʔAdaqtł*, or Pachena Bay, were drowned by a tidal wave.

These days Pachena Bay is where people camp, either as they get set to start the West Coast Trail, or as they come off it. Dave and I have made good time on our last day and can't face the prospect of any more dried food, no matter how "Supreme" the label declares it to be. Bamfield is but a hitchhike away, and I have friends there who will feed and water us, hopefully with something much stronger than water. Bamfield is a charming place, the Venice of Vancouver Island as it is sometimes known, because the town is divided by Bamfield Inlet, and the only way to the west side of the town is by boat across the "canal." Much as Dave and I would love to spend another night pressed together in my tent like a couple of strands of wet pasta – rain clouds are banking on the horizon again – there's something about the prospect of hot food, cold beer, clean clothes, and dry beds that tugs a little more insistently in the direction of town. So we turn our backs on the bay.

Pachena Bay and a corner of the universe at night.

So we've hiked the WEST COAST TRAIL AND COME AWAY WITH a trove of memories, tales that will get taller with repeated telling. We'll find words to describe it all, render it somehow more real, in keeping with the tendency of our species to think of a place only in relation to our presence in it. Yet surely the power of a place like this rests with its constancy, its timelessness, its immutability, and indeed its indifference to our attempts to encapsulate, to categorize, to summarize. In *Possession* A. S. Byatt writes exasperatedly of our need to label everything, including the shore:

> *Where the salt breakers fell on the new sand*
> *With roar unheard, and curling crest unseen*
> *Like nothing else, for no man-mind was there*
> *To name, or liken them, in any way.*
> *They were themselves alone, and rose and fell*
> *Changing-eternal, new, not knowing time*
> *Which their succession measures for the mind.*

Carmanah Beach: the waves are "themselves alone."

I stop for a moment and turn back toward the bay for one last look. I hold my breath for one last listen. I clear my "man-mind" of its clutter, and for a moment I'm suffused with a sense of wonder at what nature has put on offer.

Then I have this crazy notion. Should I bow? Dave is over in the clearing, fiddling with his camera. He won't notice. The hike is over and I can't help feeling some sort of punctuation is in order, some sign of appreciation. I'd tip my hat if I was wearing one, but short of that I toy with the idea of performing a reverential bow, complete with backpack. Then it occurs to me that perhaps I should *take* a bow of self-congratulation. Not for having survived the trek, although I sure do feel a sense of achievement, but more as an emissary of a species that for once had the collective intelligence to pull back from the brink and preserve this place.

Nah, I think, suddenly embarrassed. Instead I turn and yell something to Dave about Bamfield and beer. We traipse out of the clearing and cadge a lift to town. But later that night, and even today, I can still hear the surf, the ocean's rapturous and heartfelt applause. The West Coast Trail is, even now, calling "Encore!"

Sea stacks near Carmanah Point: for once, we had the intelligence to pull back from the brink and preserve this place.

THE JUAN DE FUCA MARINE TRAIL

IT IS THE LAST WEEKEND IN SEPTEMBER AND A FEW BRAVE SOULS are still working their way along the West Coast Trail, falling into Bamfield and Port Renfrew as another season winds down. Dave and I are also straggling toward Renfrew aboard his dubious pickup-cum-camper, although this time the object of our curiosity is not our familiar West Coast Trail, but its provincial cousin, the Juan de Fuca Marine Trail. It is a miserable day, so foul and distempered a Saturday morning that even a visit to Mom's Cafe in Sooke, and the downing of one of their legendary breakfasts, has failed to warm our bodies or our mood.

On the road to Renfrew, it's a three-foot day as we drive past Jordan River, and the surfers are out, slick and black like seals in their head-to-toe wet suits. We pass China Beach, the eastern trailhead for the Juan de Fuca Marine Trail, and it takes us another 45 minutes to drive the length of the trail, through Port Renfrew, and into the parking lot at Botanical Beach.

Though the surf was only moderate back at Jordan River, we are anticipating big waves out here at the western extremity of the trail. Just a couple of days earlier, three tourists were swept to their deaths on Long Beach by a rogue wave, so Dave is hoping to put together a rogue's gallery at Botany Bay. Then we will go sample the new trail.

Botany Bay. No self-respecting Australian can be unmoved by the prospect of a trip to any place called Botany Bay, even if this one is half a world away from its more famous namesake where Captain James Cook first made landfall in Australia more than two centuries ago. Cook had talked up the place in his dispatches, but when the First Fleet arrived there 18 years later, "The dry buzzing monotony of the landscape did not match Cook's account." Or so writes Robert Hughes in *The Fatal Shore*. Hughes continues, "The bay was open and unprotected, and the Pacific rollers gave it a violent, persistent swell."

So, too, at Botany Bay, British Columbia. While there's certainly nothing dry about the landscape here, nor is it monotonous, Pacific rollers are smashing against the back of a sea stack, and there is such a mighty sonic boom as they hit a low shelf that you'd swear the beach is shaking. Out here, facing the storm's blast, it's a six-foot day – although there is nothing along this shore to tempt a surfer.

Logs 30 feet long are flicked back and forth in the waves like mere twigs. A small bay filled with sea foam resembles a cup of cappuccino filled to overflowing. A river otter exits the salal near the shore and picks its way over to the water and disappears into the soup.

All the while, Dave urges me closer to the edge of a rock ledge, seeking that definitive rogue wave shot that will make him famous and me fish food. We compromise on a moderately adventurous pose (we both get wet), and make our way back to the Botanical Beach parking lot, where the Juan de Fuca trail begins or ends, depending on which way you hike.

The recently constructed parking lot is plastered with signs, one of which boasts of B.C. Parks' "Quality Service Guarantee." I wonder if that means they'll repair Dave's muffler while we go for a hike. There is also a lengthy dissertation on the park rules, including a system of self-registration for campers and a fee, $6 per party per night, and a penalty of $58 if you get caught in a tent without paying. There is some bureaucratic babble about what constitutes a "party" in the view of B.C. Parks. I don't have a slide rule to figure out if that means Dave and I, but then we're not going to camp at Botanical, anyway. We decide on a

Weathered stone beaches epitomize the Juan de Fuca Trail experience.

Adding a little bounce to my cable-bridge crossing.

short hike in to check it out, after which we'll strike out on the hike proper.

We wander down to Botanical Beach along a wide trail of compacted gravel, a real day-tripper's track. Botanical Beach used to be a slog to get to – no fancy road, no fancy parking lot, and a rough trail down to an isolated beach where you were unlikely to see anyone else. It's a wonderful beach, still, although the ease of access afforded by the new trail means it is no longer as exclusive as it once was.

A couple of middle-aged tourists labour up the hill toward us, frantic at having sighted a black bear. Dave and I seek out what I have recently seen referred to as "charismatic mega fauna." We find instead some charismatic *mini* fauna, a yearling black bear cub, near the mouth of a small stream. It is feeding on shellfish among rocks along the shoreline and seems unperturbed by our attentions. It doesn't seem the least bit anxious for its mother, and we pretend that we're not either.

But today we tool around the beach for an hour or so. The tide pools at Botanical Beach are known internationally as a natural outdoor laboratory, and researchers have identified over 230 plant species and about 101 invertebrates. An abundance of marine plants and animals are visible at low tide, when you can pick your way across weathered sandstone platforms networked with potholes and channels. Because of the time of year we miss the grey whales normally sighted in April and May, as well as the killer whales seen in the summer. It is possible to encounter a seal or sea lion settled on the rocks, but the seal grotto at Parkinson Creek is a summer place for mating and rearing and is visible only by ocean access.

The rain returns with a vengeance and puts an end to our wandering. Dave and I decide this is not the time to start hiking anywhere with fully laden packs, so we head back up to the parking lot, drive part way back down the trail, and start hiking there.

That's a very significant thing that distinguishes the Juan de Fuca Marine Trail from the West Coast Trail. Here, we can drive the length of the trail and cherry pick where we want to hike, whereas when you hike the West Coast Trail, well, you hike the West Coast Trail. No convenient road access, no nipping back to the truck for a can of pop or an umbrella.

FOLLOWING PAGE. *Stiff and sore, yet euphoric, bleary-eyed hikers greet the daybreak at an informal beach camp.*

We nip back to the truck. We drive back down Highway 14 to the next access point, at the Parkinson Creek trailhead, having shaved six miles off the 30-mile hike. Except we find nothing to hold us here either, and so we drive around a poorly constructed barrier and hightail it along an old logging road that runs parallel to the hiking trail.

At one point we encounter the genuine "mega fauna" deal in the form a good-size black bear, and when we stop under some alder trees for a few minutes, I end up in a serious staring contest with a northern saw-whet owl. Our back road adventure finally brings us down to Little Kuitshe campsite, each tent site hacked out of a recovering clearcut and complete with its own stump. And, of course, there are nicely engineered pit toilets, although no one around to use them. This would be a depressing place to arrive at after a long day slogging along the coast in the mud and rain. So, we backtrack to the highway.

At this point, it must be said, Dave and I have pretty much given up hope of having a West Coast Trail experience – or anything approximating one – on the Juan de Fuca Marine Trail. The fact that the forest was clearcut from here to Sombrio doesn't help – alder has never been much of a substitute for old-growth cedar and hemlock and Douglas fir. Some Parks bumpf refers to the "remnant" old-growth one will encounter on the trail and they're not kidding. And then there's the road. At some points you can hear trucks and cars on the road from the trail, and it just doesn't work as wilderness.

What with the weather behaving the way it is, we cannot even begin to muster the energy to seriously hike a chunk of the trail. And, anyway, Sombrio Beach beckons. We've heard it's a good place to camp and there's no way we can hike there before nightfall, so we drive.

As we dip down through a couple of switchbacks in yet another clearcut, we see about a dozen vehicles parked in the Sombrio Beach parking lot. They belong to some surfers, mainly, who are not the friendliest bunch in Creation. I wander down from the parking lot to the beach itself, dusk starting to tug at the sky and the shadows deepening along the trail. The evening calm is suddenly shattered by a

Mystic Beach: after the rain, a natural shower cascades down the cliff.

Foul weather breeds spectacular surf.

chain saw spitting into action. Apparently one of the squatters is short of firewood. The sound is rather more apt than it should be on a hiking trail, and I leave the beach to the sound of crashing waves and a gnawing saw.

We camp, then, in the back of Dave's truck. The rain lashes down as we feast on marinated steaks and pasta and demolish a bottle of 1995 Columbia Crest merlot, plus several healthy hookers of Lagavulin 16-year-old single Islay malt whisky.

In the morning, I saunter back down to the Sombrio River, which is in full flood, the colour of milk chocolate. Two downed spruce smack against each other in the torrent, giving off a wonderful drum beat. Gulls alight on the water and surf backwards on the river's surface, bobbing into the incoming waves.

At West Sombrio Beach the passage is difficult along a shoreline strewn with massive clumps of kelp flung up by the now receding storm. The tide is high and driftwood is jammed into every place where kelp isn't. I have decided to hike for a while and get a sampling of the trail, so I pick carefully along the beach, thankful not to be burdened with anything heavier than a notebook, an apple, and a granola bar.

Quickly the shore becomes impassable and I head up an alternate route cut by B.C. Parks. I climb for a while and then look back down to Sombrio, where morning surfers are framed by a couple of big spruce trees. It's an engaging scene, but I realize something is missing. While there is a strip of big trees along the shore that I've been hiking through, behind me there is no canopy at all. The trees stop abruptly and there is a desert of cloud where there should be a mantle of green. "Remnant" old-growth indeed.

In 1983 logging in a 215-acre area beside Sombrio Beach was given the go-ahead. With foresight, the Sierra Club and Greenpeace opposed it, claiming the logging would destroy irreplaceable old-growth and the area's recreational value. Unfortunately their campaign was without success. As reported in the local daily *Times-Colonist* on October 31, 1984: "A beautiful area is now actually being destroyed. In years to come, people will look back and wonder at the stupidity that allowed such an area to be logged." Looking back and forward, we do wonder indeed.

I hike on, seeking the next beach, and slide down a steep, muddy embankment to a creek that is swollen to the point that it's a thigh-high proposition to cross it. Suddenly, checking out East Sombrio Beach seems like a more urgent task than getting soaking wet, and so I retrace my steps to the Sombrio River, which is slung with a remarkably robust steel bridge.

On the east side of the river are the remnants of the Sombrio Nation. You won't find the name on a treaty claim map because the Sombrio Nation refers not to a Native community, but to a loose affiliation of consciously lost souls who came to squat here in the late 1960s and 1970s and spent a couple of decades homesteading and, in some cases, raising families.

When we visit, most of the squatters had been booted off the beach, having been evicted in 1996, two years after the marine trail was announced. Most of the driftwood and tarp shacks had been torn down by the time we arrive, but a few dwellings still remain. The residents seem to have collected everything society needs least. There is junk everywhere, much of it protected from the rain by blue tarps. For all that this place was celebrated as the largest and most permanent of British Columbia's squatter camps, it is hard to feel much sympathy in the face of such squalor.

The buildings that remain are substantial and stand on private land that B.C. Parks was not able to appropriate. Some of the most dedicated squatters live here, but they, too, are facing eviction. There is a pastoral simplicity to the scene, where a youngster wanders around with nothing on but a pair of rubber boots and a shirt, and a man with wiry greying hair sweeps the stoop. These buildings at least convey a sense of rootedness, aided by the presence of chickens, geese, and goats, and evidence of a considerable garden.

The sense of domesticity is spoiled only by the presence of chicken poop on a portion of the beach. I decide not to interview the people, whose tenure is clearly uncertain and for whom my notebook can only arouse more anxiety.

As blue sky threatens and the Olympic Peninsula begins to write its signature on the horizon, we set off for the trailhead at the China Beach parking lot, mile zero on the Juan de Fuca Marine Trail. We drive, of course.

From the parking lot, we hike the first mile of the trail back toward Port Renfrew. The hike is through a toothpick forest, straggly second-growth with a tangled understory. Our one mile gets us as far as Mystic Beach, and as we emerge from the forest, the sun does likewise from the clouds. It is a spectacular beach, and we spend a sensuous hour lolling around on the sand and photographing a wonderful waterfall that gushes from a cliff top like a natural shower. The cliffs are sculpted by waves and run through with geological strata, like massive stone layer cakes. One cliff is overhung by flowering asters.

We then head back to China Beach trailhead. Our trip has been more of a sporadic day hike with car stops than the rugged coastal adventure we had planned. Apparently the trail four miles westward to Bear Beach is worth the trek. Beyond Bear to Chin Beach is the most difficult section of the marine trail, challenging even the experienced hiker to carry a pack up and down the switchback and razorback route. And beyond that is Loss Creek, where a suspension bridge sits 200 feet above a canyon floor.

The one advantage of the Juan de Fuca Marine Trail is that, with several trailheads to choose from, you can pick parts of the trail and do them on a weekend. The trail can also be enjoyed by all level of hikers, with the more challenging parts attractive to those who are fit and prepared. While there are several compelling coves and cliffs to explore off the trail, Parks people warn that camping or hiking on unofficial sites can be risky due to rising tides and rogue waves. As well, high tides and storms may cut off beaches along the trail. Spectacular pristine wilderness the Juan de Fuca is not, but from what I hear, the beach camps and coastline passages make it a rewarding trip.

For Dave and me, though, there is only one West Coast Trail. It begins in Port Renfrew, where this trail ends. Our sampling of the Juan de Fuca Marine Trail has affirmed that there is really nothing like the West Coast Trail anywhere in the world, even right next door.

THE HOW, WHY, WHEN, AND WHERE OF
THE WEST COAST TRAIL FOR THOSE WHO DARE

IMAGINE GOING ON A WILDERNESS HIKE AND NOT TAKING ANY food. Apparently it's been done by some misguided soul who thought he could wander the West Coast Trail and live off what fish he caught along the way. The problem is that, while the waters off the West Coast Trail are rich with salmon and halibut, they're mighty hard to catch with a spinning rod off a rock when there's a force 9 gale blowing in your face and huge swells crashing at your feet. Not just hard, make that impossible. And there aren't a lot of fish in the rivers, either. Taking a path less travelled like the West Coast Trail requires exacting preparation. It's not a cakewalk, and you can't spend your way out of trouble. Once you're on the trail there's nothing to buy except ferry rides. But if you are cavalier in your preparations, you'll surely pay, for it can be a misery to be on the trail if you're not properly equipped. So, that said, here is some practical information.

The trail is open from May 1 to September 30 every year. Parks Canada experimented with extending the season for two weeks either side of those dates, for a

The author in his kitchen: not one to go far without food and fine wine.

reduced fee. They abandoned the idea "for public safety reasons," according to a spokesman for the park. "We got hammered by the weather." Since 1991 there has been a quota system to limit the number of hikers to about 8,000 a year. It pays to book in advance, and even if you don't, you have to register to get on the trail at the Parks Canada information booths at either end. If you don't get a backcountry pass, wardens have the right to kick you off the trail, which is a rotten way to end a hike. Early and late in the season it's possible to turn up without a booking and walk onto the trail the same day. At the peak of the season, during July and August, the trail is booked solid. If you just show up, you'll have to wait on average one day, although three-day waits have been known. The quota system allows 52 new hikers onto the trail every day, 26 at either end. Of those, 20 at each end are people who have booked, so only six people at either end get to start the trail each day without a booking. They're admitted on a first-come, first-served basis. A third entry point, via Nitinat Lake, was established as part of the agreement to include the three Native bands in the operation of the trail. Just eight hikers a day are allowed to join the trail via Nitinat Lake, and for this trailhead, bookings are mandatory. Parks Canada charges a combined trail and booking fee of $95 to hike the trail, no matter which trailhead you use. To book, people living in Vancouver should call 663-6000. Elsewhere in British Columbia, Canada, or the United States, call 1-800-663-6000. Overseas callers should dial whatever numbers get them connected to Canada, followed by (250) 387-1642. Bookings are accepted as of March 1 for the following season only. For people who don't book, the fee is $70, but of course you run the risk of having to wait a couple of nights to get on. Note that the maximum size for any party is 10 hikers. As a concession to schools, education groups, and nonprofit organizations, a special rate of $30 per person is offered between May 1 and May 31 only. These groups can also be larger, up to 18 members, and bookings can be made any time for these special group hikes. There is no special rate for children, since taking children under 12 years old on the West Coast Trail is discouraged. Finally, if you prefer hiking the trail with an organized tour, call the applicable number above. Parks Canada can supply you with an up-to-date list of companies from around the world that organize group tours.

Government Wharf, Port Renfrew: one end of the equation.

Once you've decided when to go, the next trick is deciding how to get there. The trail is not a circuit hike, so you can't leave your car and circle back to it a few days later. Some people just choose to hike to the Nitinat Narrows and double back to their car, but if you want to hike the whole thing and not retrace your footsteps, you have a logistics problem. It can be solved using a combination of bus services.

The West Coast Trail Express operates two bus routes daily from mid-June to Labour Day. Departures from Victoria at 7:00 a.m. provide service to the Bamfield, Port Renfrew, and Nitinat trailheads. If you're coming off the trail, this service gets you back to Victoria, departing Nitinat at 10:45 a.m., Bamfield at 1:00 p.m., and Port Renfrew at 5:00 p.m. Service to and from Nanaimo is also provided for all three trailheads. For current schedules, prices, and reservations, phone (250) 477-8700, or visit the West Coast Trail Express web site at *www.pacificcoast.net/~wcte*. Booking in advance is highly recommended, especially near the beginning and end of the season.

Some hikers drive to one end of the trail and therefore want to get back to where they started. A charter bus operates between Port Renfrew and Bamfield. The Pacheedaht Bus Service, operating out of the Pacheedaht band office, can be chartered for a minimum of $160, or simply $40 a person if there are more than four passengers, to a maximum of 10. Phone: (250) 647-5521. Fax: (250) 647-5561.

Another route into Bamfield is via Port Alberni. Western Bus Lines operates Monday through Friday from Alberni to Bamfield and return. For up-to-date arrival and departure times and fares, phone (250) 723-3341.

You can also get to Bamfield from Port Alberni aboard the MV *Lady Rose,* a charming coastal freighter that chugs down the Alberni Inlet every day except Monday and Wednesday in the summer. It takes three to four hours and is a lot more fun than driving on logging roads. It's also a great way to end a hike. The boat leaves Bamfield at 1:30 p.m. each day that it sails, except Sundays. On Sundays it runs from Port Alberni to the Broken Islands Group, then carries on to Bamfield (arriving at 1:00 p.m.), and then departs for Alberni again at 3:00 p.m. Cost: $20.00 per person each way. Phone: (250) 723-8313. Fax: (250) 723-8314.

Another, much quicker link to Bamfield is the Bamfield Express, a water taxi from Port Alberni that operates on a charter basis and takes about one and a half hours. For prices and group rates, phone (250) 728-3001 or (250) 720-9246.

Other than the above routes into Port Renfrew and Bamfield, you can drive to the head of Nitinat Lake, following signs to the Carmanah Pacific Provincial Park from Duncan or Lake Cowichan. That way you can access the newer Nitinat trailhead. Call (250) 723-4393 for details. Otherwise, you might be able to convince a long-suffering spouse or friend to drive you to one end and pick you up at the other. Or, if you're feeling flush, you can charter a plane. Or, if you're feeling flushed, hitchhike. Many people do.

There are two other rides that everyone has to take. The boat service on or off the trail at Port Renfrew is run by Butch Jack Hiker Ferry Services at (250) 647-5517. Otherwise, the only money you'll need on the trail is about $5 to cross the Nitinat Narrows. Just get to the dock and wait.

Finally, there is a marine route for getting up and down the trail. A commercial fisherman, Brian Gisborne, runs the gillnetter *Michelle Diana* as the Juan de Fuca Express water taxi during the season, offering what is billed as "a whale-friendly method of transportation" to anyone prepared to pay $75 for the run from Port Renfrew to Bamfield (about 2.5 hours), or $50 for a trip between Nitinat Narrows and Bamfield or Port Renfrew. He can be contacted at 1-888-755-6578 (toll free in B.C.), (250) 755-6578 (outside B.C.), or (250) 722-2972. He can also be found via E-mail, *juanfuca@island.net,* or visit his web site at *www.island.net/~juanfuca/*

A note of caution: over the years these services have fluctuated a bit, and they're bound to keep doing so. Times and prices will vary. The best way to check for up-to-date information is to call the information booths operated by Parks Canada at the Port Renfrew or Bamfield trailheads. In Port Renfrew, (250) 647-5434. In Bamfield, (250) 728-3234. These are the places where you register on starting a hike, and where you check out on completion. If you plan to hike and don't have a booking, they can give you an estimate of the length of time you'll have to wait to get on. They maintain daily reports on bear and cougar sightings, will give you tide tables, and will sell you maps and books. They'll even give you an update on the weather, something you can also get by calling (250) 724-1333, which is a recorded marine weather forecast. Check with Parks Canada about fishing licences if you do pack a rod. It's against the law to fish without a licence.

If the complications of booking a spot on the trail and finding your way there are too taxing, then you're probably not ready for what comes next – hiking it. In addition to being resourceful enough to get onto the trail, hikers should be prepared for the worst. That means be prepared to be injured, be prepared to find ladders out and bridges washed away, and be prepared to get wet and cold and to stay that way. Chances are none of the above will happen, but this is a rainforest and an exposed coast and it can turn nasty on you in an instant. I don't intend to provide an exhaustive equipment list, but there are some essentials.

Absolutely critical: good boots, well broken in and waterproofed and with lots of ankle support. Don't try to hike this trail in running shoes or light walking boots. Take waterproof everything. That means tent, matches, fire starters, clothing, and pack cover, as well as protection for your camera and plastic bags and waterproof stuff sacks to store dry clothes, maps, and anything else that you don't want to get wet. For yourself you'll

The MV Lady Rose *chugs out of Bamfield.*

need a synthetic sleeping bag, which is preferable to a down-filled one if it gets wet.

Take food, enough to stretch at least two days longer than you're planning to be on the trail, but not so much that you'll be eating it three weeks later. Most dried food that's available at outdoor recreation stores is palatable enough. Pack a few nuts and energy bars for eating along the route each day and make sure you have plenty of those Japanese noodle soups, which are a cinch to cook and great to slurp out of a cup while you're fussing over the main meal.

Take a first-aid kit (including moleskin for blisters and chafing), a length of rope, a flashlight, a sewing kit (for running repairs), insect repellent, water purification tablets, sunblock, lip balm, a pocketknife, and a small stove. If you're confident you can start a fire even in driving rain, you might want to leave the stove behind and cook over campfires.

All of the above should be carried in a proper backpack, fitted to your body shape and evenly packed. If you're carrying more than about 55 pounds, you're carrying too much (unless you're a gung-ho photographer, in which case, like Dave, you end up humping closer to 100 pounds). Even 55 pounds is a lot. Experienced hikers can live nicely out of a 40-pounder for 10 days, although they probably don't marinate too many steaks at that weight. Hiking without a proper pack will make the whole exercise a misery. Dave recalls seeing two people carrying a large gym bag between them stuffed with canned food. That's plain dumb. Remember, too, that if you're hiking in a group, there's no point in everyone bringing one of everything, so you can share the load and make everyone's pack lighter.

What to wear? I always hike in shorts. If it's cold, I wear long johns with shorts over top. It just frees up your legs to do what they're there for, which is to hike. If you have knobbly knees and insist upon covering your legs, lightweight pants can be had, but leave any denim at home. It chafes, and it's deadly when it's wet. In general, wearing several layers of light clothes is smarter than wearing one set of heavy clothes. Temperatures – the air temperature and your body temperature – can vary enormously between forest and sea, and between hiking and resting. So you can add or subtract layers to suit. But whatever you choose, make sure you have good rain gear

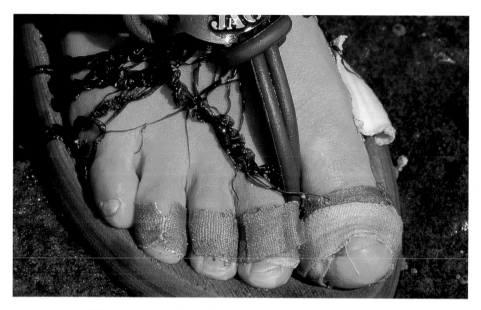

Blisters are inescapable on the trail, and a first-aid kit is a necessity.

to seal the deal. Even if you don't hike in it (too cumbersome, too hot), it'll make camping in the rain more tolerable. Another good idea is to pack a pair of running shoes or nylon and rubber beach sandals, so you can give your boots and your feet a rest around the campfire. Pack good socks, a hat, and sunglasses, plus a change of underwear if you want to end the hike on friendly terms with the rest of your group.

Standard cooking gear and utensils are all you need on the trail. Outdoor stores have all manner of lightweight pots and pans that pack nicely into tight spaces. Don't suffer the weight of an axe: there's wood everywhere for fires. Do take a water bottle and one of those nylon water bags that fold down to nothing in your pack but can hold a couple of gallons of water when scooped into a stream. Do take a map, either waterproofed or slipped into a re-sealable plastic bag, and take tide tables. These are a must: get caught on a rock shelf at high tide and your hiking days will be over. During summer months, add an hour for Pacific Daylight Saving Time to the time that appears in the tide tables. And watch for waves if you are rock hopping. The surf arrives uninterrupted from somewhere near Japan and can get awfully big sometimes.

Even with quotas limiting the number of hikers on the trail, campsites can get crowded, especially at the bottom end of the trail where there are few beaches for people to spread out. There is some basic etiquette, most of which pertains to not fouling everyone's nest. There are pit toilets at some sites and they should be used. Otherwise, the decent thing is to do your thing below the high water mark and let the sea flush it. Burn the toilet paper. As for garbage, there's simply no excuse for leaving a shred of it. Burn paper, pack out everything else. One big consideration is fresh water, especially in summer months when the streams are running low. Even if companies aren't logging upstream and mucking with the hydrology that way, there's a risk of giardia or E. coli, with attendant diarrhea and stomach cramps, due to waterborne bacteria. You can boil water, filter it, or treat it with purification tablets. The other thing to watch for is that you get your water from far enough upstream to be clear of any place people have been washing, or whatever. As for when you are washing, be conscious not to pollute the stream for whoever comes next. Use biodegradable soap, if you insist on using soap at all; that goes for dish and body soap. Frankly, though, figure that you're on a wilderness hike and you can do without a wash for a few days. Scrape your dishes clean with sand and rinse them in the ocean. In other words, leave the fresh water for drinking. Take along some soap that lathers in salt water, if you insist upon having a wash, and dunk yourself in the ocean. As for shaving, forget it. At crowded campsites it's not a bad idea to opt for one or two communal fires. It's a good way to meet people, and it means the entire campsite won't end up being one big fire pit. And so as not to attract critters, keep food stored away from your tent, preferably in a well-sealed stuff sack suspended a good distance from where you plan to sleep.

Chances are you'll have a perfectly safe, injury-free hike. On average, though, someone has to be hauled off the trail once every two days. This doesn't include the walking wounded who manage to struggle to the end of the trail. People break bones, usually because their boots fail them or they slip on ladders or boardwalks. Others suffer progressive injuries, whereby they might sprain a joint early on and it gets so sore they can't continue. Still others simply find they're not fit enough. And then there are those fingers that get caught, and sometimes lost, when people grab the wrong cable on the cable car crossings. Added to all this is the threat of hypothermia. Even during the warmest months, dense fog can shut out the sun, and if you're slicked with sweat and then stop hiking, you can cool down extremely quickly. In the wetter, colder months the problem is magnified. Wear a hat to retain body warmth, most of which goes straight out the top of your noggin. And keep soup or powdered cocoa near at hand to boil up something hot quickly if need be: a good shot of something warm in the belly can soon turn things around. If you do get injured, or someone in your party does, Parks Canada asks that you attempt to reach Thrasher Cove, Camper Bay, Cullite Cove, Logan Creek, Carmanah Light Station, Nitinat Narrows, Tsocowis Creek, or Pachena Light Station. Send a written message for help with other hikers, and be specific about what ails you. Anyone who is seriously hurt will probably be pulled out by helicopter; otherwise, by boat. Prepare to wait at least 24 hours, longer if the weather is bad. Don't leave an injured hiker alone.

Don't take pets. They're not allowed, and the ladders and other structures would make it hell for them, anyway. Wardens will not rescue injured pets. As for animals you might encounter along the way. . . well, there are bears around. Don't climb a tree, don't try to outrun one, don't cry out, and don't try to stare it down. Just attempt to retreat quietly and calmly. There are also cougars on the trail, which tend to attack children or crouching adults, especially around dawn and dusk. Again, just back off slowly. And never leave children alone. Otherwise, none of the creatures you'll encounter should pose any risk, except perhaps for shellfish. Paralytic shellfish poisoning is a real risk, and Parks Canada also worries that with so many hikers on the trail, harvesting shellfish will put whole populations at risk. So they discourage the eating of shellfish.

Finally, leave enough room in your pack to take a book, preferably this one. The only other book worth the freight, and it's a worthy accompaniment, is the Sierra Club's guidebook, *The West Coast Trail and Nitinat Lakes* (Douglas and McIntyre), which gives a useful blow-by-blow description of the trail, and whose map is a handy supplement to the one put out by Parks Canada.

As with the West Coast Trail, the Juan de Fuca Marine Trail poses logistical challenges, although they are minor by comparison. The main hitch is common to both – getting on and off the trail. The solution is much the same, too. The Pacheedaht First Nation, which operates the bus service between Port Renfrew and Bamfield, also operates a service between Port Renfrew and Sooke. It has four departures a day from either end. In the case of the West Coast Trail, of course, the bus service only operates between trailheads. However, since the Juan de Fuca Marine Trail runs parallel to Highway 14 and has numerous points of access, the Pacheedaht bus service functions as a "milk run" between them. Botanical Beach, Parkinson Creek, Sombrio Beach, China Beach, Jordan River, and Sooke are all on the schedule. The cost of a full trip from Renfew to Sooke is $16; trips between other stops cost from $2 to $13.

Oh, yes, one last point. When you do hike the big one, the West Coast Trail proper, take the most important thing of all: time. You can hike the trail in five days, although you'll see little more than your boots. The West Coast Trail is really a 10-day hike, allowing for a couple of days of gambolling around on the beach unencumbered by your pack. If that's too much time out of a hectic schedule, a week is okay. Anything less is doing yourself a disservice. Then again, you can always go back. We sure intend to.

The Natives dry salmon on the coast, while hikers dry their footwear, which seldom tastes as good.

Lthough the Pacheedaht, Ditidaht, and Ohiaht people share much in the way of history, territorial boundaries, and political affiliation, they are not so readily grouped by language. The Pacheedaht and the Ditidaht speak slightly different dialects of the same language, called Nitinaht. It is a language in the South Wakashan subgroup of the Wakashan language family. The Ohiaht, on the other hand, speak a dialect of Westcoast (sometimes known as Nootka). While it is in the same subgroup of the Wakashan family, Westcoast is a quite different tongue than Nitinaht, such that the Ohiaht spoken language is quite incomprehensible to the Ditidaht and Pacheedaht, and vice versa. The written languages are quite similar, however.

Detailed orthographies have been produced by Randy Bouchard of the British Columbia Indian Language Project, and by Eugene Arima, et al. (see reference below). They are not reproduced in full here. Rather, the special characters that appear in Native place names used in the text are explained below. Diligent readers are welcome to try to pronounce the names based on the information provided. It isn't easy.

One of the distinctive characteristics of these Native tongues is their use of

Cleared for landing: cormorants near Carmanah Point.

glottalization, a sort of stopping sound for which there is no real equivalent in English. In the word *Ch'ibataqsɫ*, for example, the sign *Ch'* represents a glottalized *ch*. The same effect pertains to the following characters:

P' as in *P'aachiidˀ*, is a glottalized or cracked sound.

ˀ at the end of the same word is a glottal stop or "catch," as in "uh-uh."

ts' at the end of *ˀO:yats'*, is glottalized.

Other characters denote the following:

x̣ as at the end of *P'aachiidˀaaˀtx̣*, is a sound drawn into the back of the throat, or uvula, as in the German *ach*.

aḳ at the end of the word *Waayaaˀaḳ*, is an uvular *k*.

O: as in *ˀO:yats'*, is a long vowel, as are all other vowels that are followed by a colon; simply pronounce them longer.

ˀ̣ as in the word *Ho:ˈ:i:ˀatḥ*, is a laryngealized glottal stop, which means it is made with the back of the tongue retracted toward the back wall of the throat.

ḥ at the end of the same word, is like an *h* far back in the throat.

ɫ as in *Ch'ibataqsɫ*, is a voiceless or unsingable *l*.

tɫ as in *ˈAdqatɫ*, is like the *ɫ* in *Ch'ibataqsɫ* (see above), but with an initial stopping of breath, then release.

Readers who want to know more about the language characteristics of the West Coast people are referred to *Between Ports Alberni and Renfrew: Notes on West Coast Peoples*, E. Y. Arima et al., Canadian Ethnology Service, Mercury Series Paper 121, Canadian Museum of Civilization.

Two fascinating unpublished but publicly available reports are *Indian Knowledge and Use of the Walbran, Logan, and Cullite Creek Watersheds* and *Preliminary Notes on Ditidaht Land Use*, both prepared by Randy Bouchard and Dorothy Kennedy of the British Columbia Indian Language Project. The reports can be found in the library of the archaeology branch of the provincial government's Ministry of Small Business, Tourism, and Culture.

Photographer Dave Nunuk made repeated trips to the West Coast Trail, typically with about 40 pounds of camera gear added to his backpack. He made two types of trips: ones where he would hike the entire trail, and therefore need a full complement of food and equipment; and trips where he would get a boat or helicopter ride in and set up a base camp, thus allowing him to carry extra camera gear.

When Dave hiked the whole trail, his camera gear was usually comprised of the following: film – 40 rolls of Fujichrome 35 mm Velvia 50 ASA and Ektachrome 100 Elite; cameras – Nikon F3, Nikon 801S, Nikon FM; lenses (Nikon, unless otherwise specified) – 20 mm $f3.5$, 28 mm shift, 55 mm $f2.8$ macro, 80-200 $f4$ zoom, 300 mm $f4$, plus extension tubes; filters – an assortment of graduated neutral density filters and polarizers to control contrast, but no colour filters. Dave also carried cable releases, a Vivitar 285 flash, a Manfrotto ART055 tripod with ball-and-socket head, plus a Manfrotto clamp for shooting at ground level. He took an extra tripod head for 8- to 10-hour night exposures.

On short trips Dave carried a little more: cameras – Canon F1 and two Nikon FE2s for night shooting; lenses – two 28 mm $f2.8$ lenses, a 105 $f2.5$, a 300 mm $f4$ with a 1.4 times converter, a Canon 500 mm *f*4.5 with 1.4 and 2 times converters. The star photography was done with a motor-driven equatorial mount and a 12-volt battery pack. The mount allowed Dave to line up one axis with the north celestial pole, mount a camera, and track the stars so that over a 20-minute exposure the stars would be rendered as points of light rather than become star trails. This equipment allows the stars to be exposed just as the naked eye sees them in the sky.

Stars exposed just as the naked eye sees them in the sky. To get this shot, the photographer used an equatorial mount, and took his time.